AF394525

High Times Singles 1992-2006

" God Bless Our
High Times…"

© 2007 by International Music Publications Ltd
First published by International Music Publications Ltd in 2007
International Music Publications Ltd is a Faber Music company
Bloomsbury House
74–77 Great Russell Street
London WC1B 3DA

Arrangements: Alex Davis
Editor: Lucy Holliday

Cover Photography by David Hughes.
Book Photography: James Dimmock, Rick Guest,
Chris Lopez and Rankin.
Art Diection: JK, Jon Cooke & Seb Marling
Design: Pete Richardson for Village Green

Printed in England by Caligraving Ltd

ISBN10: 0-571-52861-9
EAN13: 978-0-571-52861-5

To buy Faber Music publications or to find out about the full range of titles available,
please contact your local music retailer or Faber Music sales enquiries:

Faber Music Ltd, Burnt Mill, Elizabeth Way, Harlow, CM20 2HX England
Tel: +44(0)1279 82 89 82   Fax: +44(0)1279 82 89 83
sales@fabermusic.com   fabermusic.com

WHEN YOU GONNA LEARN

Words and Music by Jason Kay

Fm9
Em9
8
us here. Ar - ma - ged - don's come too near, too, too near
in the sea, greed - y men been kil - ling all the life there ev - er was.

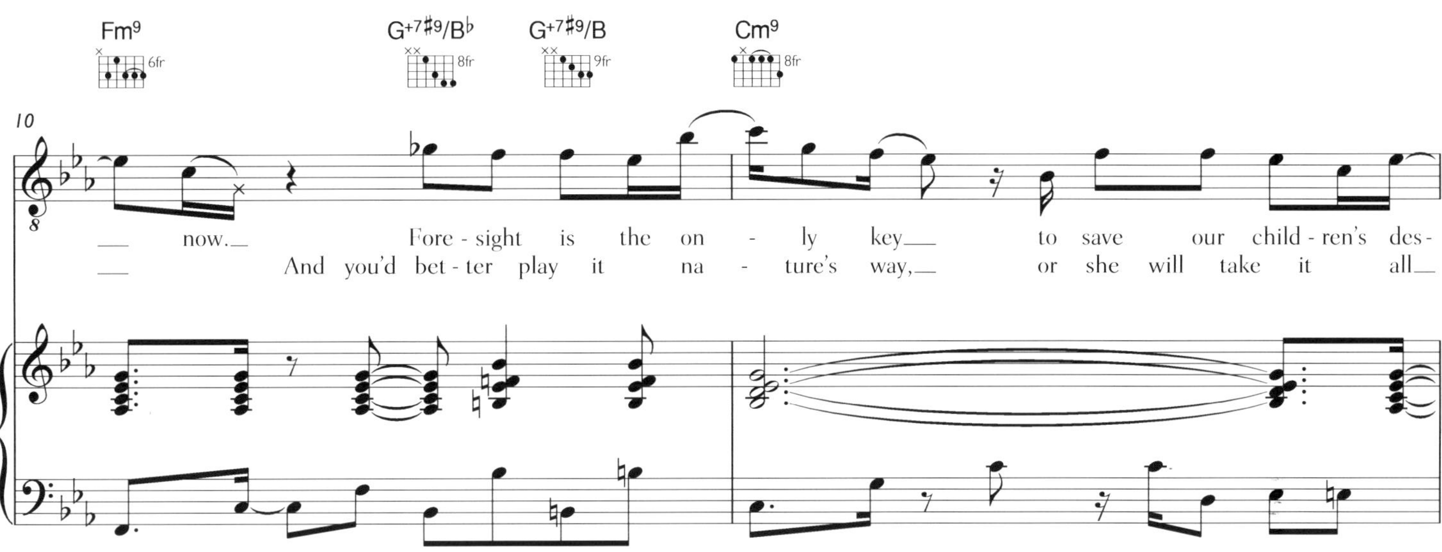
Fm9
G+7#9/Bb
G+7#9/B
Cm9
10
now. Fore - sight is the on - ly key to save our child - ren's des -
And you'd bet - ter play it na - ture's way, or she will take it all

Fm9
Em9
12
- ti - ny. The con - se - quen - ces are so grave, so, so grave
a - way. And don't try and tell me you know more than her 'bout right from wrong.

Fm9   G+7#9/Bb   G+7#9/B   Cm7
14
___ now.___ The hy-po-crites, we are___ their slaves, so my friends to stop
___ Oh you've up-set___ the ba-lance, man,___ done the on-ly thing___

Fm9   Em9   Fm9   G+7#9/Bb   G+7#9/B
16
___ the end, on each o-ther we___ de-pend, on___ we___ de-pend.
___ you can. Now my life is in___ your hands.

Abmaj7/Bb   Dm9   Dbmaj7   Cm9
19
Moun-tain high and ri-ver deep.
Moun-tain high and ri-ver deep, oh___ yeah. We've got-ta
ff

D♭maj7   Fm9   A♭maj7/B♭
22
Stop it go - ing on.
stop it go - ing on.
We got - ta wake this world up
Dm9   D♭maj7   Cm9   D♭maj7   Fm9
To Coda
24
from its sleep.   Oh peo - ple,   stop it go - ing on.
27
Didgeridoo solo
Bass Guitar
mf
Cm9   Fm9
Ah, hey.   Ah,
Em9   Fm9   G+7♯9/B♭   G+7♯9/B   Cm9
37
hey.   Ah, hey.

D.% al Coda

Fm9
Em9
Fm9
G+7#9/B♭   G+7#9/B
Ah, _______ hey. _______________________ Ah

Coda
A♭maj7/B♭
Dm9
D♭maj7
Greed - y men_ will fade___ a - way,_   yeah,_ yeah, yeah,

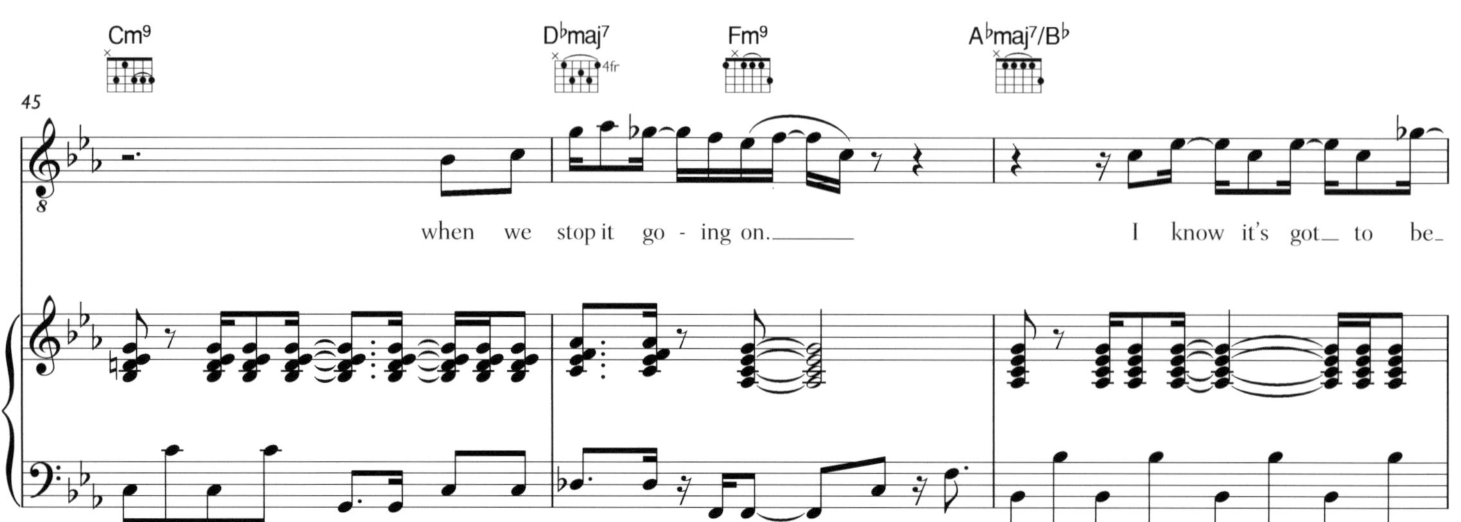
Cm9
D♭maj7
Fm9
A♭maj7/B♭
when we stop it go - ing on.________   I know it's got_ to be_

Dm9 Dbmaj7 Cm9 Dbmaj7 Fm9
that way. Oh peo - ple,_ stop it go - ing on._ I'm ask - ing,
Abmaj7/Bb Dm9 Dbmaj7
oh, when you gon - na learn_ to stop it go - ing on?_
Cm9 Dbmaj7 Fm9 Abmaj7/Bb
_ Now when you gon - na learn_ to stop it go - ing on?_ Now when you gon - na learn
Dm9 Dbmaj7 Cm9 Dbmaj7 Fm9
Repeat & ad-lib. vocals to fade
_ to stop it go - ing on?_ Oh when_ you gon - na learn_ to stop_ it go - ing on?_

TOO YOUNG TO DIE

Words by Jason Kay
Music by Jason Kay and Toby Smith

world, yeah, all a-round the world,___ have seen their bro - thers___ fry. I seen your bro-ther fry.
What's the mo - tive in their
mad - ness? Oh I___ wish___ I knew.___ You made_ my peo - ple cry.___ You made my peo-ple cry.
So po-li - ti - cians,_ this time, I think you bet-ter keep your dis -

A♭maj7/B♭   A♭maj9   Gaug7#9   %   Cm9   D♭m9
28
- tance.___   Say,___   say it loud,   we're too young to   do do   do__ do__   da da
Fig. 1
A♭m9   B♭m9   Cm9   D♭m9   A♭m9   B♭m9
31
do do da da do_______ do.   Do do do_ do_____ da da   do da_ da do.___
Fig. 1
Cm9   D♭m9   A♭m9   B♭m9   Cm9   D♭m9
34
Do do do_ do__ da da   do da da do_______ do.   Do do do_ do_____ da da
Fig. 1
A♭m9   B♭m9   To Coda   Cm9   F9(add6)
37
do da__ da do.___
Fig. 1
f
mp

A♭maj7/B♭
A♭maj9
F/G
41
Yo, here's a mes-sage...
(C)
44
2. All__ gone__ when they drop the bomb, can the po-li-ti-cians re-as-sure?__ 'Cause
(F)
46
here I am__ pre-su-ming that no-bo-dy wants__ a war.__ There's so
(B♭)
(A♭)
(G)
48
ma-ny peo-ple pray-ing just to find______ out if they're stay-ing but
(C)
50
late-ly state-ly gov-ern-ments and dis-il-lu-sioned lead-ers so
(F)
52
full of emp-ty pro-mi-ses but rare-ly do__ they feed us. Put our

(B♭)
(A)
(B♭)
(B)
backs a - gainst the wall,________ or don't__ we count at all?_________ Can
Cm7(add4)
you de - cide,__ are you mes - me - rised,__ do you know which side you're stand - ing? 'Cause
Gm9/F
when it falls__ gon - na take us all,__ got - ta know what we're de - mand - ing. I
B♭m9
Am7
Am11
D.% al Coda
ne - ver lie,__ can't you hear the cry__ co - ming from on high?_ We're too young to die.

Coda
Cm9   D♭m9   A♭m9   B♭m9
8fr   9fr   4fr   6fr
62
Do do do do do,   da da do___ do,___   da da do__ do.__
Backing vocals sing Fig. 1

Cm9   D♭m9   A♭m9   B♭m9
8fr   9fr   4fr   6fr
64
Ah don't you know__ you're too young___ to die,__ yeah.__ Oh I'm too

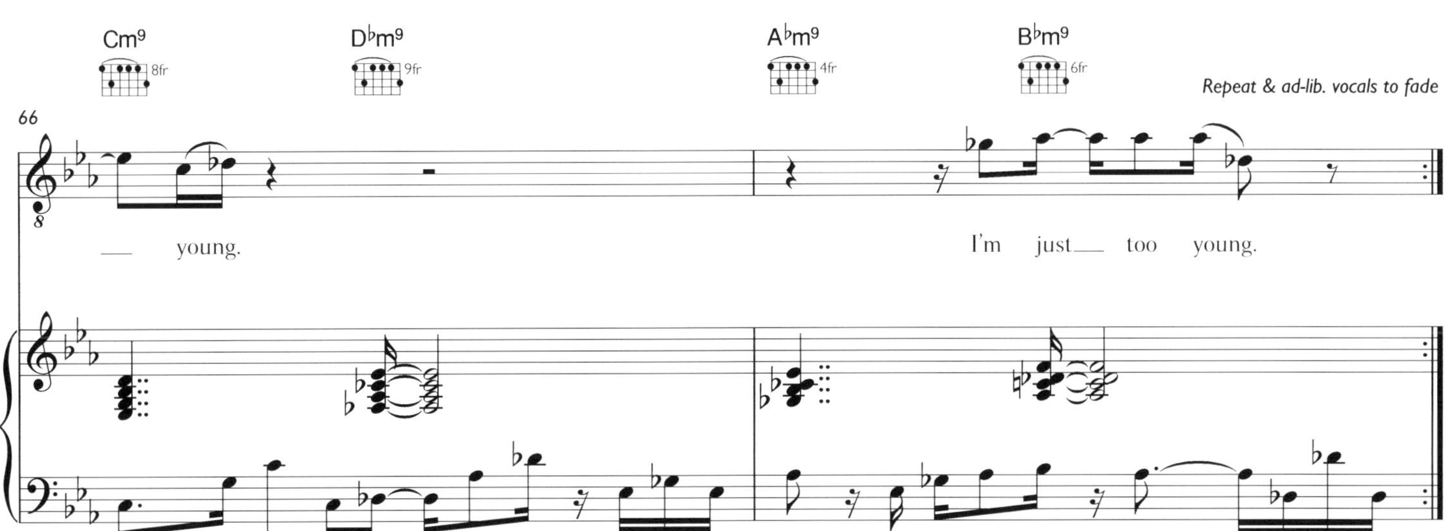
Cm9   D♭m9   A♭m9   B♭m9
8fr   9fr   4fr   6fr
Repeat & ad-lib. vocals to fade
66
__ young.   I'm just__ too young.

BLOW YOUR MIND

Words and Music by Jason Kay and Toby Smith

Dm9
Em7(add4)
Am(maj7)
E♭m9
Fm7(add4)
-ny - thing, I need you. Ba da
mf
B♭m(maj7)add6
E♭m9
Fm7(add4)
B♭m(maj7)add6
da, ba da da, ba da da ba da da da do do do do do do do do do
E♭m9
Fm7(add4)
B♭m(maj7)add6
E♭m9
Fm7(add4)
do, dip do do do do a-do do do do,
B♭m(maj7)add6
Dm9
Em7(add4)
Am(maj7)
(horns)
oh now.
1. Love ya. I need ya.
2. Plea - sure. Pas - sion. To-
3. Fe - ver. Hot now.
mp

Dm9
Em7(add4)
Am(maj7)
23
I think I wan-na squeeze__ ya.
Night-
-night's the night I'm look-ing for your ac - tion.
I want__
Help me wipe the sweat a - way__ from my brow.
Se -
Dm9
Em7(add4)
Am(maj7)
Dm9
Em7(add4)
25
- ly, so tight-ly,
girl you know you real-ly blow__ my mind.
__ to hold__ you,
don't you know that now you blow__ my mind?
- xy oh la - dy,
don't you know this time you blow__ my mind?
Am(maj7)
Ebm9
Fm7(add4)
Bbm(maj7)add6
28
__
__
__
1.2. Say it a - gain just one__ more time,_ I've got
3. Oh,____ don't you know, yeah,__ don't_
Ebm9
Fm7(add4)
Bbm(maj7)add6
31
__ to know__ how you came__ to blow__ my mind.__
__ you know__ by now that now you blow__ my mind,__ yeah._

E♭m9
Fm7(add4)
B♭m(maj7)add6
To Coda
1.
E♭m9
(3° only)
Clo - ser.
Oh yes, you do, yes, you do, yes
2.
D♭m9
Fmaj9
Cmaj9
E♭m9
D♭m9
Fmaj9
Cmaj9
Horns
Horns
f
f
E♭m9
D♭m9
Fmaj9
Cmaj9
D.S. al Coda
Coda
E♭m9
Fm7(add4)
B♭m(maj7)add6
(yes) you blow my mind.

Dm9
Em7(add4)
Am(maj7)
Dm9
Em7(add4)
Am(maj7)
Dm9
Em7(add4)
Am(maj7)
Dm9
Em7(add4)
Am(maj7)
Ebm9
Fm7(add4)
Bbm(maj7)add6
Ebm9
Fm7(add4)
Bbm(maj7)add6
Trumpet and scat-style vocal line sung in "do's"
44
47
50
53

E♭m9
Fm7(add4)
B♭m(maj7)add6
56

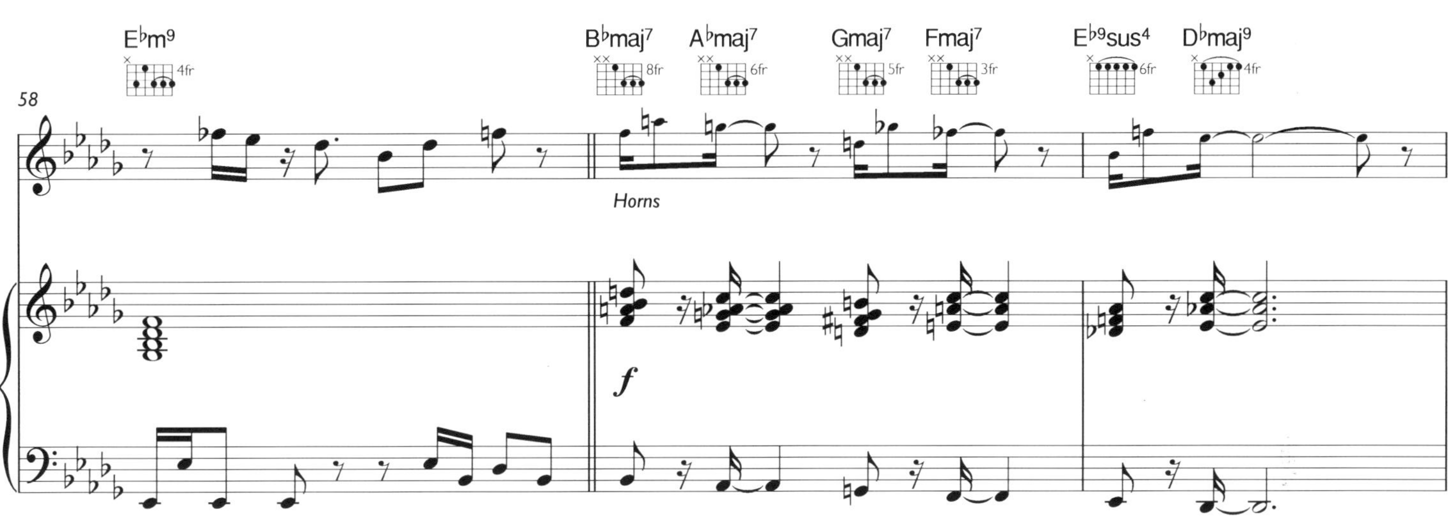
E♭m9
B♭maj7
A♭maj7
Gmaj7
Fmaj7
E♭9sus4
D♭maj9
58
Horns
f

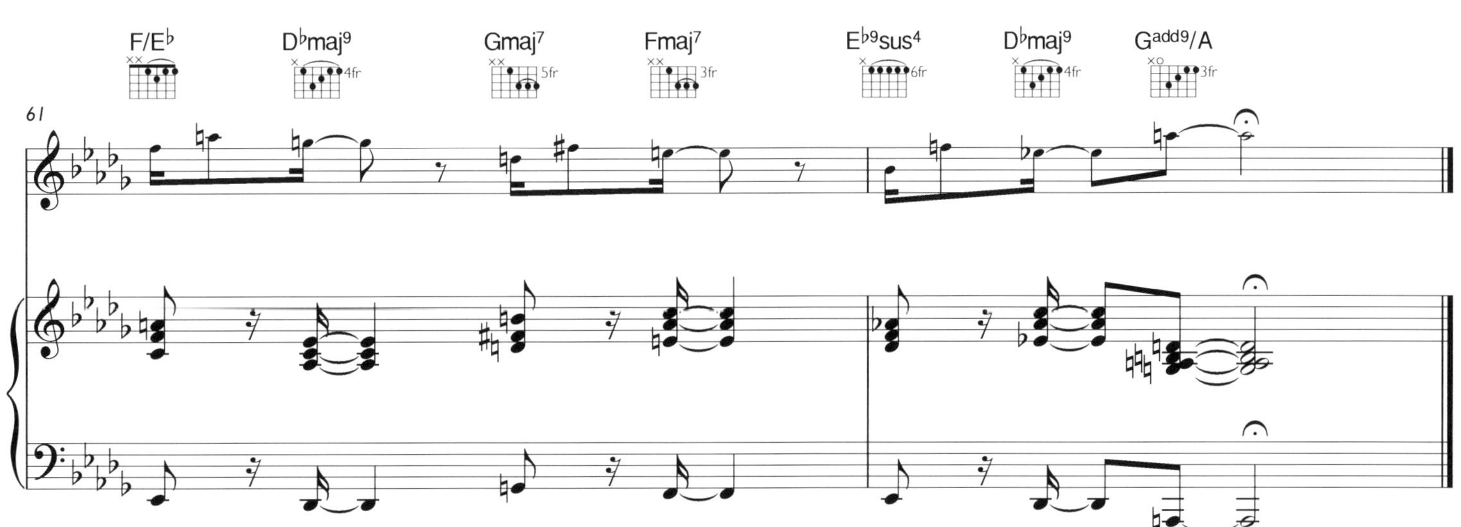
F/E♭
D♭maj9
Gmaj7
Fmaj7
E♭9sus4
D♭maj9
Gadd9/A
61

EMERGENCY ON PLANET EARTH

Words and Music by Jason Kay and Toby Smith

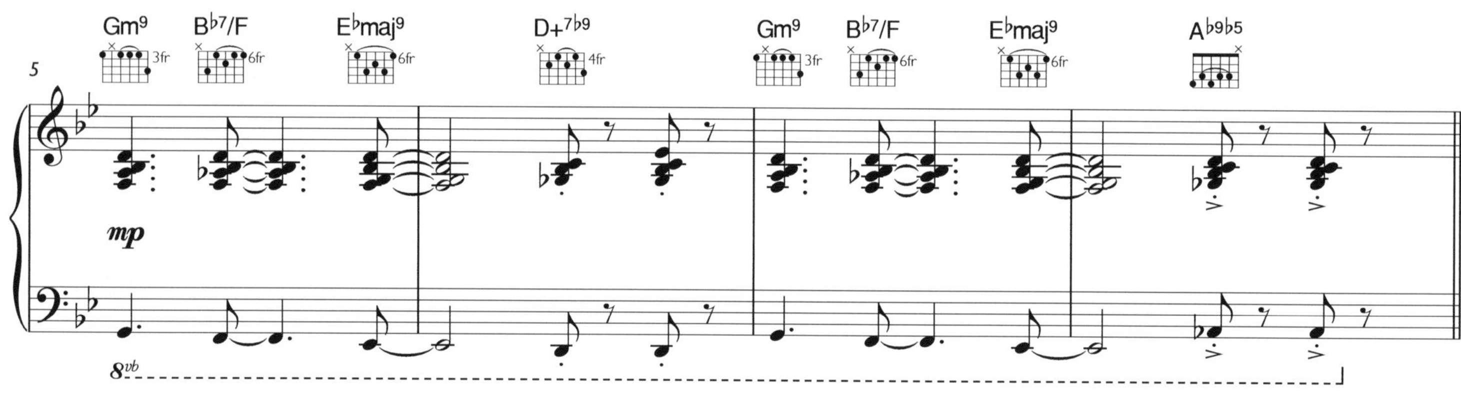

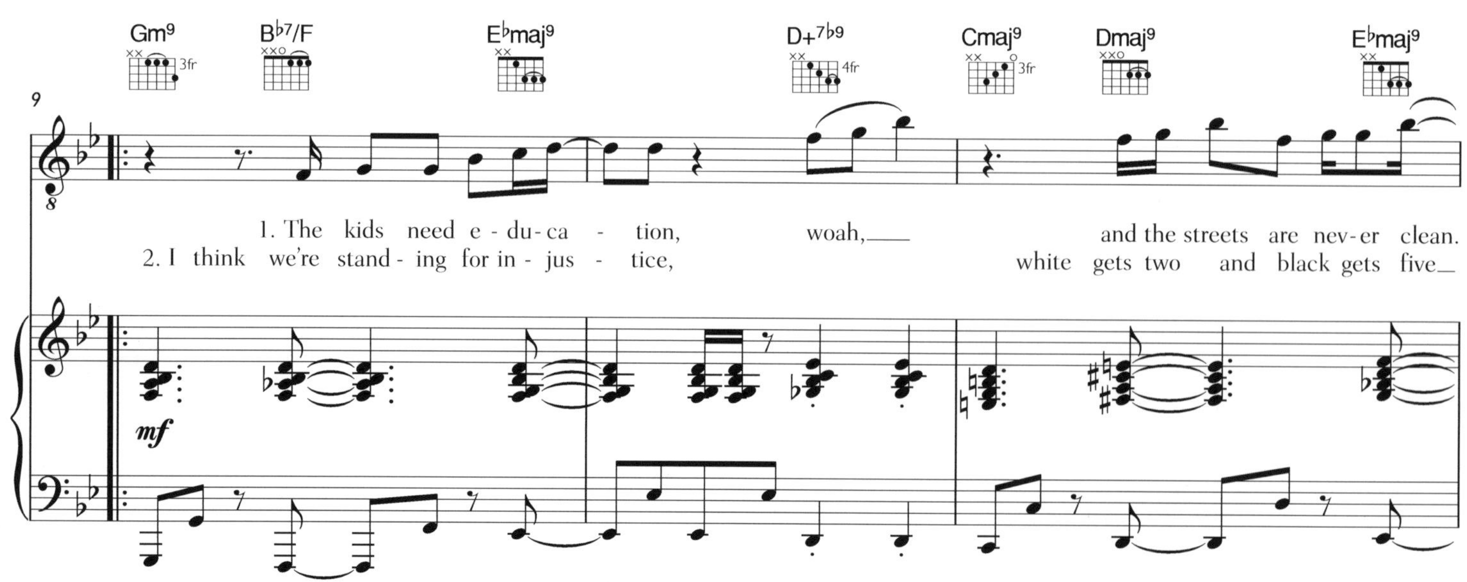

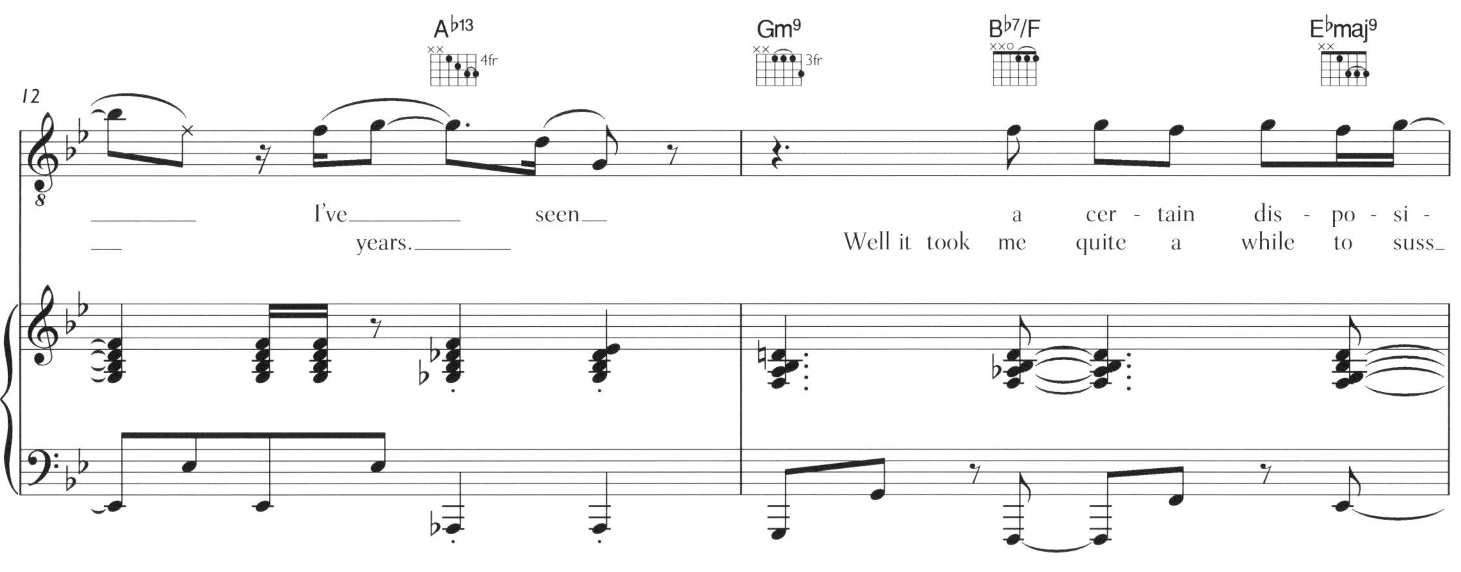

A♭13
Gm9
B♭7/F
E♭maj9
4fr
3fr
I've_______ seen___
a cer - tain dis - po - si -
___ years._______
Well it took me quite a while to suss_

D+7♭9
Cmaj9
Dmaj9
E♭maj9
A♭13
4fr
3fr
4fr
- tion
pre - vail - ing in the wind,___
sweet_ change.
___ this.
Now I know_______
my head is clear.___

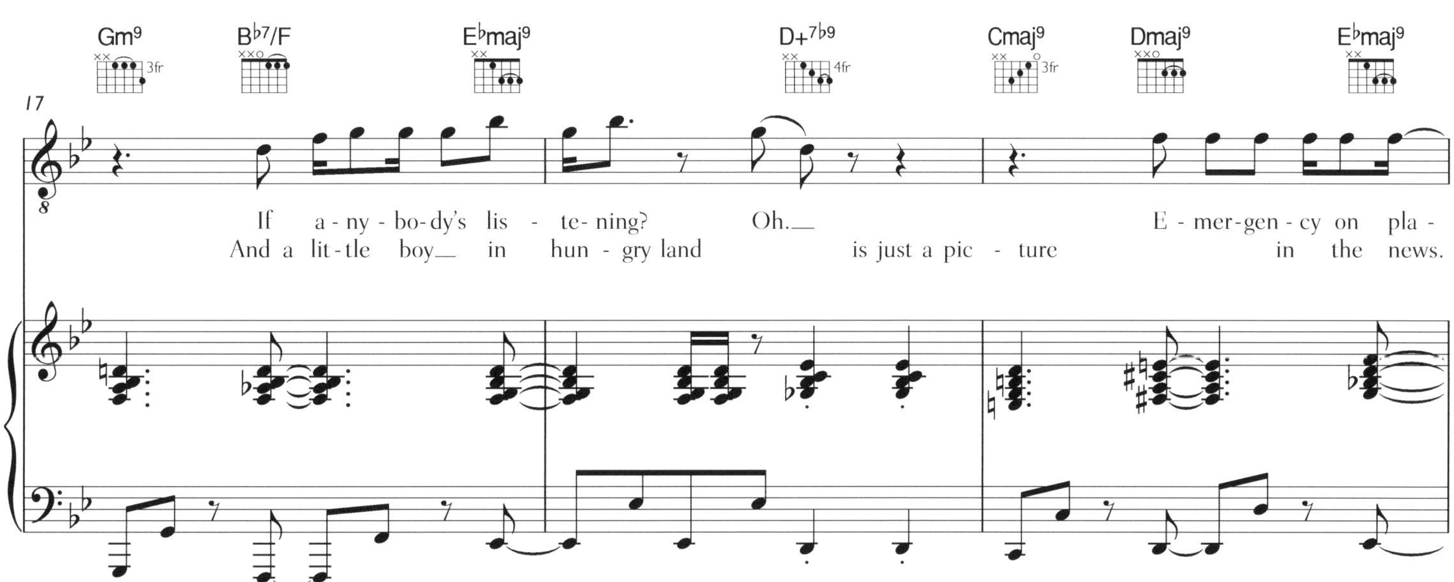

Gm9
B♭7/F
E♭maj9
D+7♭9
Cmaj9
Dmaj9
E♭maj9
3fr
4fr
3fr
If a - ny - bo - dy's lis - te - ning?
Oh.___
E - mer - gen - cy on pla -
And a lit - tle boy_ in hun - gry land
is just a pic - ture
in the news.

A♭13 Gm9 B♭7/F E♭maj9 D+7♭9
- net Earth.___
Is__ that life__ that I am wit - nes- sing?___ Or just_ a - no-
___ Won't see him in the T. V. ad-ver-ti - sing__ 'cause it__ might
Cmaj9 Dmaj9 E♭maj9 A♭13 Gm9 Am9 B♭m9
- ther wast - ed birth?___
put you off your food___ now yeah.
Now we got e - mer-
Cm9 Dmaj9 E♭maj9 A♭13 D♭maj9
- gen - cy,___ oh___ we got e - mer - gen - cy__ on pla - net Earth.
Gm9 Am9 B♭m9 Cm9 Dmaj9 E♭maj9
Oh now we got e - mer - gen - cy,___ oh___ we got e - mer - gen - cy__ on pla-

A♭9sus4 D♭maj9 B♭9sus4 E♭maj9 Gm9 Am9 B♭m9 Cm9
- net Earth. Yes we have. Is a-ny-bo-dy out there?
2° Come on!
Dmaj9 E♭maj9 A♭13 D♭maj9 Gm9 Am9 B♭m9
Is a-ny-bo-dy out there? Is a-ny-bo-dy out
Cm9 Dmaj9 E♭maj9 A♭9sus4 D♭maj9 B♭9sus4 E♭maj9
there yeah? Oh____ we've got e-mer-gen-cy__ on pla - net Earth. Yes we have.
1.
(G) (A) (B♭) (C) (D) (E♭) (A♭) (D♭)
(play 2° only)

2.
(D)   (E♭)   (A♭)   (D♭)   (B♭)   (E♭)
Gm9   B♭7/F   E♭maj9
45
Is some-one out_

D+7♭9   Cmaj9   Dmaj9   E♭maj9   A♭13
48
_ there?   Yeah.   E - mer-gen-cy on pla - net Earth is what_ we got._   Come and get_

Gm9   B♭7/F   E♭maj9   D+7♭9   Cmaj9   Dmaj9   E♭maj9
51
_ me,   oh,_   some-bo - dy   help me.   Come on_ some-bo-dy help_ me now.

A♭13   Gm9   Am9   B♭m9   Cm9   Dmaj9   E♭maj9   A♭13
54
String solo

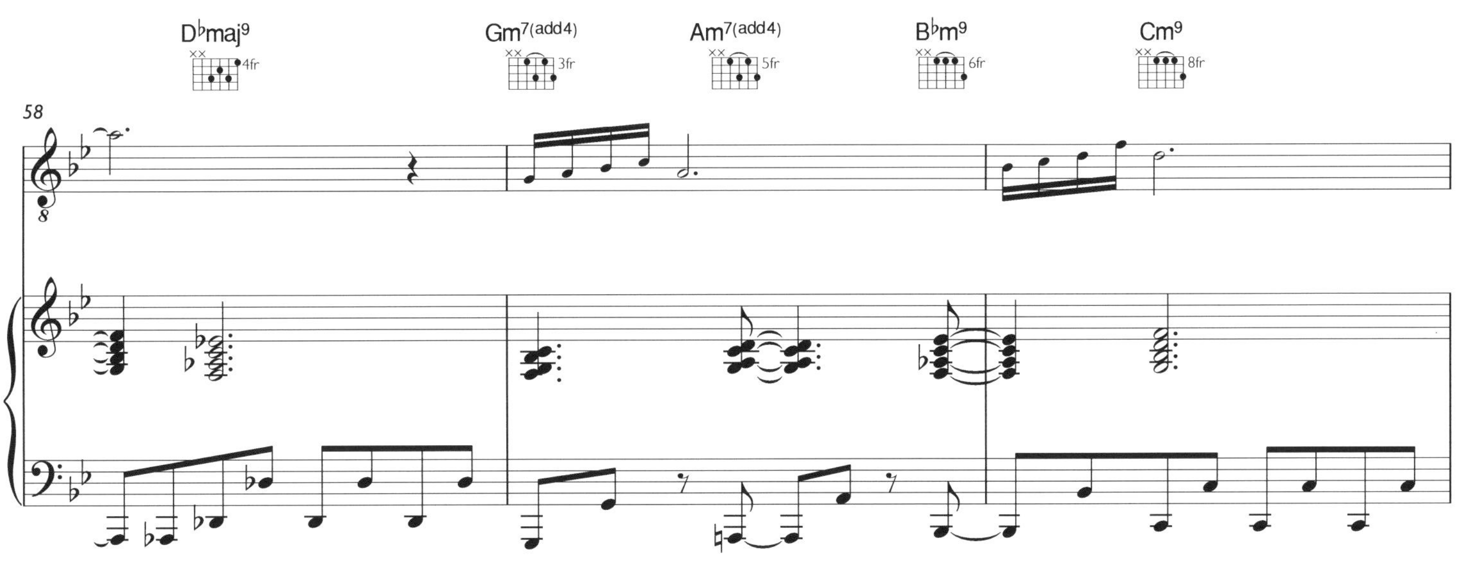
D♭maj9
Gm7(add4)
Am7(add4)
B♭m9
Cm9
58

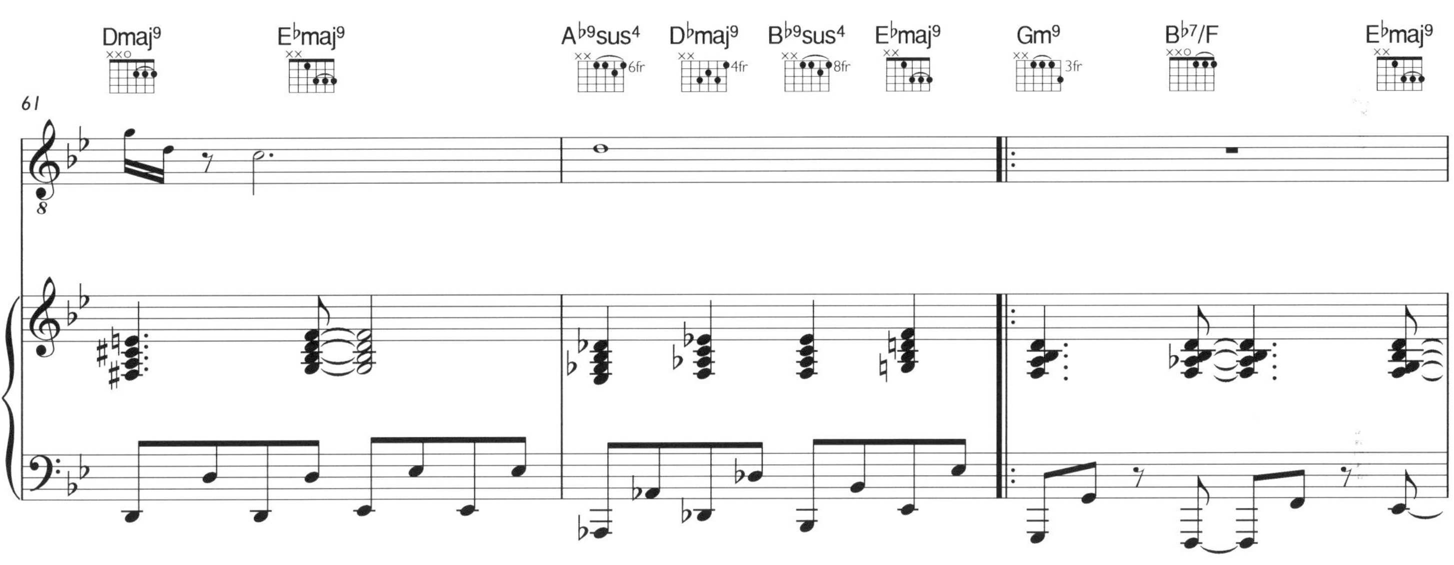
Dmaj9
E♭maj9
A♭9sus4
D♭maj9
B♭9sus4
E♭maj9
Gm9
B♭7/F
E♭maj9
61

D+7♭9
Cmaj9
Dmaj9
E♭maj9
A♭13
Repeat ad lib. to fade
64
Come on___ some-bo-dy help___ us now,___ yeah, yeah. Oh, we need___ you...

SPACE COWBOY

Words and Music by Jason Kay

Dbm9/Gb   Ab9sus4   Dbm9   Cbmaj7
10
di - sap - peared with-out__ a trace. I'm glad, oh___ I found some-
hap - pi - ness__ to shade his eyes. He's glad, oh___ that he found,___ ooh, some-
Ab9sus4   Ebm9   Fm9   Bbm9
13
- bo - dy who I can re - ly___ on.) This is the__ re - turn___ of the space cow-
- bo - dy who he can re - ly___ on.)
mp
Ebm9   Fm9   Bbm9   Ebm9
16
- boy. In - ter - pla - ne - ta - ry good__vibe zone.__ Say__ at the speed of Chee -
Fm9   Bbm9   Ebm9   Fm9
1.
19
- ba, oh you and I__ go deep - er. May-be I'll have to get__high to get by,__ hey.__
Hey___ now,_ may -

22
(A♭)
8
mf
8ᵛᵇ
Hmm, I   got that Chee-ba Chee-ba vibe.
25
2/4
(8)
E♭m⁹   Fm⁷   A♭⁹sus⁴
4fr   8fr   6fr
29
2/4
4/4
8
mp
Ah   ah   ah   yeah.   2. Ev - 'ry - thing_ is
2.
E♭m⁹   Fm⁹   B♭m⁹   E♭m⁹
4fr   6fr   6fr   4fr
32
8
(may)-be I'll have to get_ high_   just   to   get   by,_   hey._   You_

Fm9
Bbm9
1.2.3.
Ebm9
4.
Ebm9
34
Ad-lib. lead vocals
and I. You and I. You Hey!
Fm9
Bbm9
Ebm9
Fm9
Bbm9
1.
Ebm9
37
2.
Ebm9
Fm9
Bbm9
1.
Ebm9
41
Ad-lib. lead vocals
Ba ba ba ba ba ba da ba.
Ba ba da ba da ba ba ba.
Fm9
Bbm9
Ebm9
2.
Ebm9
44
Ba ba ba ba ba ba da ba.
Ba ba da ba ba ba ba ba ba.
Ba ba da ba da ba ba ba ba ba

47
Fm9
(A♭)
1.
ba ba ba.
f
8vb
51
2.
Get-ting high.   Oh,   get-ting high
(8)
A♭(add4)
C(add2)/A♭
54
yeah.   Oh this is the re-turn of the space cow-boy.   In-ter-pla-ne-ta-ry good vibe zone.
8vb
E♭m9
Fm9
B♭m9
E♭m9
57
This is the re-turn   of the space cow-boy.   In - ter-pla-

Fm9 Bbm9 Ebm9 Fm9 Bbm9
-ne-ta-ry good vibe zone.__ Say__ at the speed of Chee-ba, oh__ you and I__ go deep-
Ebm11 Fm11 Bbm11 Ebm9
-er.__ Hey__ now we'll go deep-er. Oh,__ now we'll go deep-er. You and I,__
Fm9 Bbm9 Ebm9
__ you and I,__ you and I,__ you and I,__ you and I,__
Fm9 Bbm9 Ebm9
Repeat to fade
__ you and I,__ you and I,__ you and I,__ you and I,

VIRTUAL INSANITY

Words and Music by Jason Kay and Toby Smith

Bb+7 Ebm7 Ab9
____ be do- ing for__ us.__ And I'm giv- ing all__ my love__ to this__ world__
Db9 Gbmaj7 Cm7b5 Cbmaj7 Bb+7 Ebm7
__ on- ly to be told,__ I can't see, I can't breathe, no____ more will we be.__ And
Ab9 Db9 Gbmaj7 Cm7b5
no- thing's gon- na change the way__ we live 'cause we can al- ways take but ne- ver give. And
Cbmaj7 Bb+7 Ebm7 Ebm7 Ab9
now that things are chang- ing for__ the worse see, woah, it's a cra- zy world we're liv- ing in.

42
And I just can't see that half of us immersed in sin is all we have to give these
fu - tures made of vir - tu - al in - sa - ni - ty. Now
al - ways seem to be gov - erned by this love we have for
use - less, twist - ing all the new tech - no - lo - gy. Oh now

Cbmaj9
Bb7/D
Ebm7
Abm7
Bb7
To Coda
there is no sound for we all live un-der-ground. 2. And I'm think-
Ebm7
Ab9
Db9
Gbmaj7
-ing what a mess we're in. Hard to know where to be-gin. If
Cm7b5
Cbmaj7
Bb+7
Ebm7
I could slip the sick-ly ties that earth-ly man has made. And now
Ab9
Db13
Gbmaj7
Cm7b5
Cbmaj7
Bb+7
ev-'ry mo-ther can choose the col-our of her child, that's not na-ture's way.

E♭m7   A♭9   D♭9   G♭maj7
Well that's what they said yes-ter-day.___ There's no-thing left to do but pray.
Cm7♭5   C♭maj7   B♭+7   E♭m7   A♭9
___ I think it's time I found a new_ re-li-gion. Woah_ it's so_ in-sane to
D♭13   G♭maj7   Cm7♭5   C♭maj7   B♭+7
D.℠ al Coda
syn-the-size_ a-no-ther strain. There's some-thing in_ these fu-tures that_ we have_ to be_ told.
Coda   E♭m7   A♭m7   B♭+7   C♭maj9   B♭7/D
(all) live un-der-ground, woah. Now there is___ no___ sound

E♭m7   A♭m7   B♭+7 C♭maj9   B♭7/D
if we all___ live___ un-der-ground.___ And now it's vir-tu-al in-sa-ni-ty,
E♭m7   A♭m7   B♭7 C♭maj9   B♭7/D
for-get your vir-tu-al re-a-li-ty,___ oh.___ There's no-thing so bad___
E♭m7   A♭m7 B♭7 C♭maj9   B♭7/D   E♭m7   A♭m7 B♭7
___ as a mad-hap-py man. Oh yeah, I know___ yeah.
E♭m7   A♭9   D♭9   G♭maj7   Cm7♭5   C♭maj7   B♭+7
Ooh.___
mp
6/4

Fu - tures made of vir - tu-al __ in - sa - ni-ty. Now al - ways seem to be
go-verned by __ this love we have for use - less, twis - ting all the new tech - no - lo - gy. Oh now
__ there is __ no sound __ for we all __ live un - der - ground, oh. __

Cbmaj9
Bb7/D
Ebm7
Abm7
Bb7
Ad-lib. lead vocals
Liv-ing in
vir - tu - al in - sa - ni - ty.
Cbmaj9
Bb7/D
1. Ebm7
Abm7
Bb7
Liv-ing in
vir - tu - al in - sa - ni - ty.
2.
Ebm7
Abm7
Bb7b9
Cbmaj9
Bb7/D
Ebm7
Db/F
vir - tu - al in - sa - ni - ty.
Vir-tu-al in - sa - ni - ty is
Fb/Gb
Gb
Cbadd9
Cm7b5
Cbmaj7
Bb+7
rit.
what we're liv-ing in.
Yeah...
ad lib.
mp

COSMIC GIRL

Words and Music by Jason Kay and Derrick McKenzie

Em7
F#m7
B7b9(b13)
12
___ that she was from a - no - ther time.___ Like some
asked her for her num - ber all___ the same.___ She said,
Em7
F#m7
B7b9(b13)
14
ba - by Bar - ba - rel - la___ with the stars___ as her um - brel - la,___ she
"Step in my trans - por - ter so I can te - le - port ya
Em7
F#m7
B7b9(b13)
16
asked me___ if I'd like to mag - ne - tise.___ Do I have
all a - round my hea - ven - ly bo - dy." Oh, this could
Em7
F#m7
B7b9(b13)
18
___ to go___ star trek - king 'cause it's you___ I should be check - ing, so she
be a close en - coun - ter, I should take care not to floun - der.

Em7
F#m7
B7b9(b13)
la - zer beamed__ me with__ her cos - mic eyes.__ Oh__ now.
Sends me in - to hy - per - space when I see__ her pret - ty face.
G#m7
F#m7
B7
C#m7
She's just a cos - mic girl,__ oh__ yeah,
f
G#m7
F#m7
__ from a - no - ther ga - la - xy.__ My heart's at__ ze - ro__
B7
C#m7
G#m7
F#m7
__ gra - vi - ty.__ She's from a cos - mic world.__
Woah__ wah

B7
C#m7
Put-ting me_ in ec - sta - cy,_______ ooh.__ Trans-mit-ting on_ my fre-
wah wah.
G#m7
F#m7
B7
C#m7
1.
- quen - cy._____ She's cos-mic.
Woah_ wah wah wah.__
Em7
F#m7
B7b9(b13)
Em7
Synth. solo
Guitar rhythm as in verse
F#m7
B7b9(b13)
Em7
F#m7
B7b9(b13)

Em7
F#m7
B7b9(b13)
2.
2. I'm
(G#) (F#) (B) (C#)
Sends me in-to hy-per-space when I see her pret-ty face. Sends me in-to hy-per-space
(play 1° only)
1. 2.
N.C.
G#m7 F#m7
when I see her pret-ty face. when I see her pret-ty face.
B7 C#m7
She's just a cos-mic girl,___ from a-no-ther ga-

G#m7
F#m7
B7
C#m7
- la - xy.
Trans-mit-ting on her fre - quen-cy,
yeah
G#m7
F#m7
cos - mic,
oh.
Ah can't you be my cos - mic wo - man?
B7
C#m7
G#m7
F#m7
I need you, I want you
to be
B7
C#m7
Repeat ad lib. to fade
my cos - mic girl for the rest of time.
Oh.

ALRIGHT

Words and Music by Jason Kay, Toby Smith and Rob Harris

Dm9   Am9   Cm9
Gm9   Dm9   Am9
Cm9   Gm9   Dm9
Am9   Cm9   Gm9
take me there.
to my pa - ra - dise.
I feel your sun
Sum - mer in your smile,
start to glow,
well it makes me feel
and I know it, let me show you that I
so real. (So real.) You
want your love, I need your touch for the rest of our time
tell me things and my heart sings to the world from is-lands in
to - ge - ther ba - by.
the sky.
Come fly with me e - ter - nal - ly, you and
Take my hand, as one we will stand, you

Dm9
Am9
Cm9
1.
me,   we were meant___ to be.___
know it's now or never   to say   hel-lo to for-e-ver.} Yeah   hey,   al - right.
f

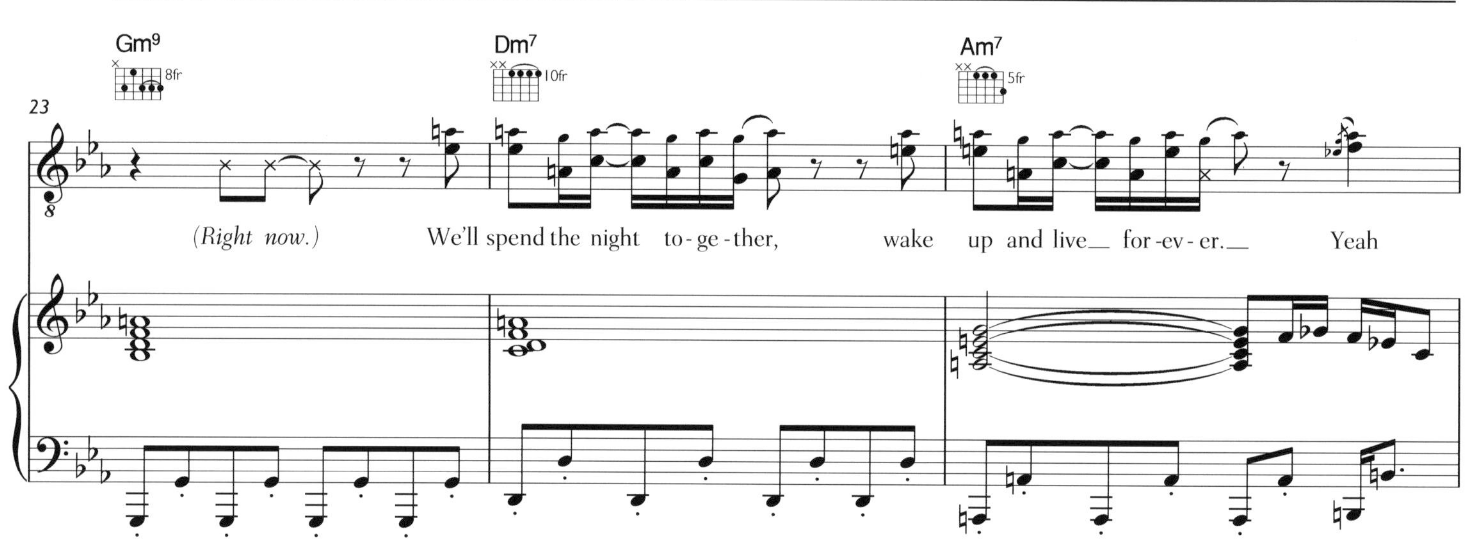
Gm9
Dm7
Am7
(Right now.)   We'll spend the night to-ge-ther,   wake   up and live___ for-ev-er.___   Yeah

Cm9
Gm9
Dm7
hey,   al - right.________ (Right now.)_   We'll spend the night to-ge-ther,   wake

Am7
Cm9
8va
up and live for - ev - er. Yeah hey. Ooh,
mf
Gm9
Dm7
Am7
(8)
ooh, ooh, oh. It's al - right now.
2.
Cm9
Gm9
hey, al - right. (Right now.) We'll
f
Dm7
Am7
Play section x4
spend the night to - ge - ther, wake up and live for - ev - er. Yeah

58
Cm9 8fr
Gm9 8fr
Dm7 10fr
38
hey.
Am7 5fr
Cm9 8fr
41
I need your touch, I want
Gm9 8fr
Dm7 10fr
Am7 5fr
43
your love so much. Ooh.
Cm9 8fr
Gm9 8fr
Dm7 10fr
46
I need your touch, and I want your love so

Am7
Cm9
Gm9
__ much. I real - ly need__ it, oh__ now, to - night. We'll
Dm7
Am7
spend the night__ to - ge - ther,__ wake up and live__ for - ev - er.__ Yeah
Cm9
Gm9
hey, al - right. (Right now.)__ We'll
Dm7
Am9
Repeat to fade
spend the night__ to - ge - ther,__ wake up and live__ for - ev - er.__ Yeah

HIGH TIMES

Words and Music by Jason Kay, Toby Smith, Stuart Zender and Derrick McKenzie

Em7(add4)   Bb7sus4   Asus2   Gm7(add4)   Em7(add4)   Bb7sus4

main - line.___   Now just gimme some of that.   And her hun - ky   fun - ky
de - xy - drene.   And when   the phone rings   you___ think

Asus2   Gm7(add4)   Em7(add4)   Bb7sus4   Asus2   Gm7(add4)

jun - ky___   of a boy - friend   got her on   late nights   with her skirt up tight.
bad things.   Well these are high,   high,   high, high   times___ yeah.   In a - ny

Em7(add4)   Bb7sus4   Asus2   Gm7(add4)

Woah___   she's   a wild___ thing.   Oh,___   let - ting it all___ swing.
back___ street,   when you take a hot___ seat,   make___ sure you   check your

Em7(add4)   Bb7sus4   Asus2   Gm7(add4)   Em9   A7b9

God   bless   our   high   times.   Don't you know that   last night   turned to day - light,   and a
flight times.   Woah now ma - ma.

Fm9
Em9
Fm9
Em9
27
min-ute   be-came a day.________   Last night   all__ my trou-
A7b9
Fm9
Em9
Fm9
30
- bles,___   well they seemed__ so   so far a - way.________   Oh________   I'm
Em9
A7b9
Fm9
33
search-ing   my re-flec - tion_   for a glimpse___ of   a - no-ther me.
Em9
Em9
A7b9
To Coda
36
___   I've   got to get a - way___ from all__ these   high________ times, 'cause these high

39
Fm9
Em9
N.C.
N.C.
Em7(add4)
Bb7sus4
times
are kil-ling me.
Guitar solo
Asus2
Gm7(add4)
Em7(add4)
Bb7sus4
Asus2
Gm7(add4)
43
Em7(add4)
Bb7sus4
Asus2
Gm7(add4)
Em7(add4)
Bb7sus4
46
Asus2
Gm7(add4)
Em7(add4)
Bb7sus4
Asus2
Gm7(add4)
Em7(add4)
Bb7sus4
49
Now drop it this time.

P - P - Pa - ra - noi - a___ will des - troy___ ya.___ P - P - Pa - ra - noi -
- a___ will___ des - troy ya. P - P - Pa - ra - noi - a___ will___ des -
- troy___ ya. Pa - ra - noi - a. Pa - ra - noi - a, this time.
got to get a - way___ from all___ these high___ times,___ woah,___ 'cause they sure

Em9
Em9
are kil - ling me. Woah, la la la la la
A7b9
Fm9
la. High times, oh
Em9
Em9
yeah. Ooh, we're li - ving in high,
A7b9
Fm9
Em9
high times yeah.
f

DEEPER UNDERGROUND

Words and Music by Jason Kay and Toby Smith

D5
F#5 E5 C#5
23
wreck it down__ yeah.
D5
F#5 E5 C#5
25
1,%. Some-thing's come to rock__ me and I can't keep my head, I get ner-vous in the
(2.) pock - et full of mon-ey and an eye full of hate, take a pleas-ure in de-
D5
F#5 E5 C#5
27
New York cit-y streets,__ where my le - ga - cy treads, I know I'm bet - ter off
-struc-tion of the ver-y thing__ that they tried to cre - ate, some-bod - y tell me why does
D5
F#5 E5 C#5
29
stand-ing in the shad - ows,__ far from hu - mans with guns,__ but now
all man - kind,__ on - ly tam - per and touch, have a hab - it where they

31
D5
F#5 E5 C#5
it's too late, there's no es-cape from what they have done. Come on.
bite off more than they can chew and now it's too much.
33
C#m
Am/C Am
I'm go-ing deep-er un-der-ground,
To Coda
35
E D/A C#m/G# C#m
there's too much pa-nic in this town. I'm go-ing deep-er un-der-ground,
37
Am/C Am E D/A C#m/G#
there's too much pan-ic in this town.

C#m
Am/C
Am
1.
I'm go-ing deep-er un-der-ground, and I've got to go
E
D/A
C#m/G#
C#5
D5
deep-er got to go much deep-er yeah.
F#5
E5
C#5
D5
They're gon-na wreck it down yeah,
F#5
E5
C#5
D5
Scat til *

47
F#5 E5 C#5 D5
* Hey yeah we're gon - na bring it down___ yeah.
49
F#5 E5 C#5
2.
Am/C Am
2. Some peo - ple with a ___
51
E D/A C#m/G# C#m
there's too much pa - nic in___ this town.___
mp
53
C#/E# E7 B♭
56
C# E#m E B♭

C#5   D5   F#5   E5   C#5
I'm go - ing, I'm go - ing, I'm go - ing deep - er un - der - ground,
mf
D5   F#5   E5   C#5
2° D.% al Coda
I'm go - ing, I'm go - ing, I'm go - ing deep - er un - der - ground,
Coda
C#m
I'm go - ing deep - er un - der - ground.
Am/C   Am   E   D/A   C#m/G#
Repeat to fade

CANNED HEAT

Words and Music by Jason Kay

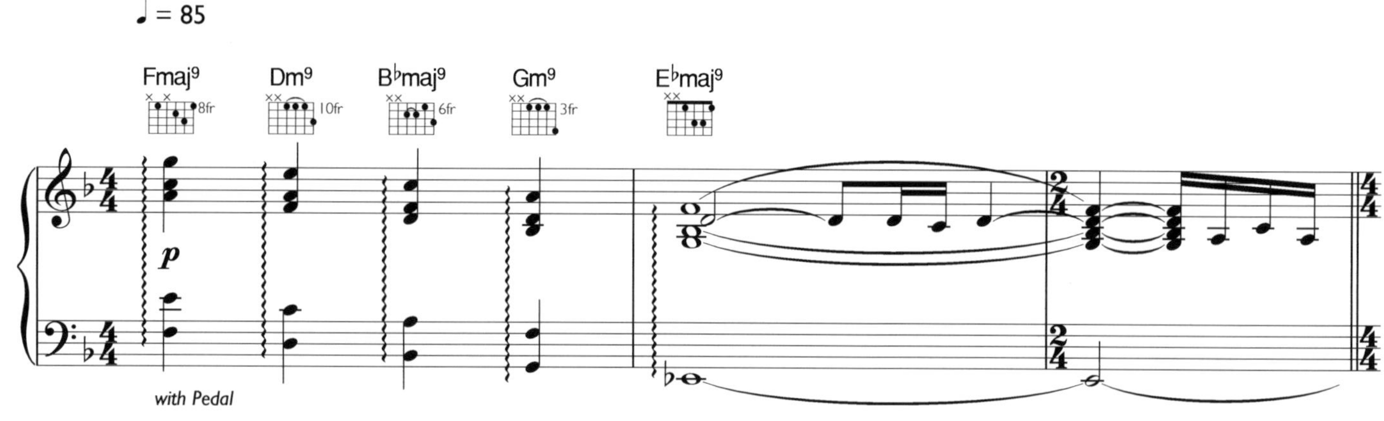

%. Dm9   Am9   B♭m9
10fr   5fr   6fr
f
1. I used to put my faith in wor - ship,
2. I feel the thun - der, see the light - ning,
%. On - ly the wind can know the ans - wer,

Am9   Gm9
5fr   3fr
but then my chance to get to Heav - en slimmed.
I know this an - ger's Heav - en sent.
and she cries to me when I'm a - sleep. She says you

Am9   B♭m9
5fr   6fr
I used to wor - ry a - bout the fu - ture,
I've got to hang out all my hang - ups,
know that you can go much fas - ter,

Bm9   Cm9   C#m9
7fr   8fr   9fr
but then I threw my cau - tion to the wind.
'cause on the boo - gie I feel so hell - bent, hey, hey.
and oth - er peo - ple's talk can be so cheap hey, hey.

Dm9
Am9
Bbm9
I had no rea - son to be care free, no, no, no,
It's just an in - stant gut re - ac - tion that I get.
I've got this voo-doo child in - grained on me.

Am9
Gm9
un - til I took a trip to the oth - er side of town, yeah, yeah, yeah.
I know I've nev - er ev - er felt like this be - fore. I don't
I'm gon - na use my pow - er to as - cend. You know I've

Am9
Bbm9
You know I heard that boo-gie rhy - thm, hey,
know what to do, but then that's no - thing new. Stuck be-
got these bur - ning heels to use, so sure there's no way I'd lose. I was

Bm9
Cm9
C#m9
I had no choice but to get down, down, down, down.
-tween hell and high wa - ter, need a cure to make it through, hey.
born to rock, and built to last, you ne-ver see my feet 'cause I move so fast.

Dmaj9 Bbmaj7 Gm9 Bb/C Dmaj9 Bbmaj7
26
Dance,   wooh,_   no-thing left_ for me_ to do_ but dance,   all these
Dance, yeah,
Dance, yeah, hey,
ff

Gm9 Bb/C Dmaj9 Bbmaj7 Gm9 Bb/C To Coda
29
bad times_ I'm go-ing through,_ just dance.   Got canned heat in my heels_ to-night,

1. Dmaj9 Bbmaj7 Gm9 Bb/C   2. Dmaj9 Bbmaj7 Gm7
32
ba - by,   wooh,____ oh ho ha.   ba - by,   you know I got canned heat in my heels.

Dm9
D.S. al Coda
36
You know_ this boo - gie is for real.____________
mf

Coda
Dmaj9 Bbmaj7 Gm9 Bb/C N.C.
ba - by, dance.
Dmaj9 Bbmaj7 Gm9 Bb/C Dmaj9 Bbmaj7 Gm9 Bb/C
Hey D. J. let the mu-sic play, I'm gon-na live this par-ty life.
Dmaj9 Bbmaj7 Gm9 Bb/C Dmaj9 Bbmaj7 Gm9 Bb/C
Hey D. J. throw my cares a-way, I wan-na live this par-ty life.
Dmaj9 Bbmaj7 Gm9 Bb/C Dmaj9 Bbmaj7
Hey D. J. let the mu-sic play, I'm gon-na live this par-ty life.

Gm9   Bb/C   Dmaj9   Bbmaj7   Gm9   Bb/C   Dmaj9   Bbmaj7
Hey D. J. throw my cares a-way, I wan-na live this par-ty life.
Gm9   Bb/C   E   Am7   C/D
You know this boo-gie is for
E   Am7   E
real, got so much canned heat in my heels, gon-na
Am7   C/D   E   Am7
Repeat to fade
dance, gon-na dance my blues a-way to-night.

LITTLE L

Words and Music by Jason Kay and Toby Smith

F⁷sus⁴
B♭⁹sus⁴
Em⁷
-ping out   'cause you can't de-cide   what you real - ly want_from me.___
- ler - ing.   How_ could this love be-come_ so_ pa - per thin?_
Play section 2° only
E♭m⁷
A♭(add2)
F⁷sus⁴
B♭⁹sus⁴
You're play-ing so hard   to   get.   You're mak-ing me sweat   just   to
Em⁷
E♭m⁷
A♭(add2)
hold_ your at - ten - tion.   I   can't give you no - thing more   if   you ain't_
F⁷sus⁴
B♭⁹sus⁴
Em⁷
E♭m⁷
A♭(add2)
___ giv - ing no-thing to me.   Don't you know_ that?
1. Why   does   it
2. You   make   me

F7sus4
Bb9sus4
Em7
Ebm7
Ab(add2)
24
Hand claps
have to be like this?
I can ne-ver tell.
'Cause you make me
love you, love you_ ba-by
with a lit-tle L.
Why does it

F7sus4
Bb9sus4
Em7
Ebm7
Ab(add2)
28
Hand claps
love you, love you_ ba-by
with a lit-tle L.
Seems like you're
have to be like this?
I can ne-ver tell.

F7sus4
Bb9sus4
Em7
Ebm7
Ab(add2)
32
Hand claps
step-ping on the pie-ces_
of my bro-ken shell.
'Cause you make me

F7sus4
Bb9sus4
Em7
36
love you, love you
with a lit-tle L__ you know,
that's the way_ you make me love you yeah.

Synth. solo
Why does it have to be like this?
I can ne - ver tell.
Hand claps
You make me love you, love you_ ba-by
with a lit - tle L.
Hand claps
Repeat ad-lib. vocals & fade

LOVE FOOLOSOPHY

Words and Music by Jason Kay and Toby Smith

Em7
Cmaj9
She got a pro-mise of love struck fas - ci - na -
She car - ries sweet-ly in - fec - tious ma-gic form -
Bm7
Em7
- tion, ooh. What am I to do? How am I
- u - las. I'm so de - li - ri-ous,
Cmaj9
Bm
to know who you are? When this
is she that se - ri-ous? Or is she bringing me on, I've been wait - ing so long. And this
Bm7
F#m7
C#m7
Em7
love fool - o - so-phy is kil-ling pre - vi-ous il - lu-sions that
I'm a love

Bm7   F#m7   C#m7   Em7
26
_ fool.   I had__ in my mind a-bout you.__   I'm a love__ fool.
f
Bm7   F#m7   C#m7   Em7
30
Seems   so true,__   all__ the lies you're tel-ling,   tra - gi-cally com-pel-ling and
I'm a love
To Coda
Bm7   F#m7   C#m7   Em7
34
_ fool.   my love__ it means no-thing to you.__   So may - be I'm still_ a love fool.
Bm7   Em7   Cmaj9   Bm7
38
Guitar plays intro part - cont. sim. til chorus
I don't__ want the world,_ I want you.
mf

Bm7
Em7
Cmaj9
(2° only)
You.
I don't
Bm7
Em7
want the world, I want you.
I want you,
I want you,
Cmaj9
Bm7
I want you,
I want you.

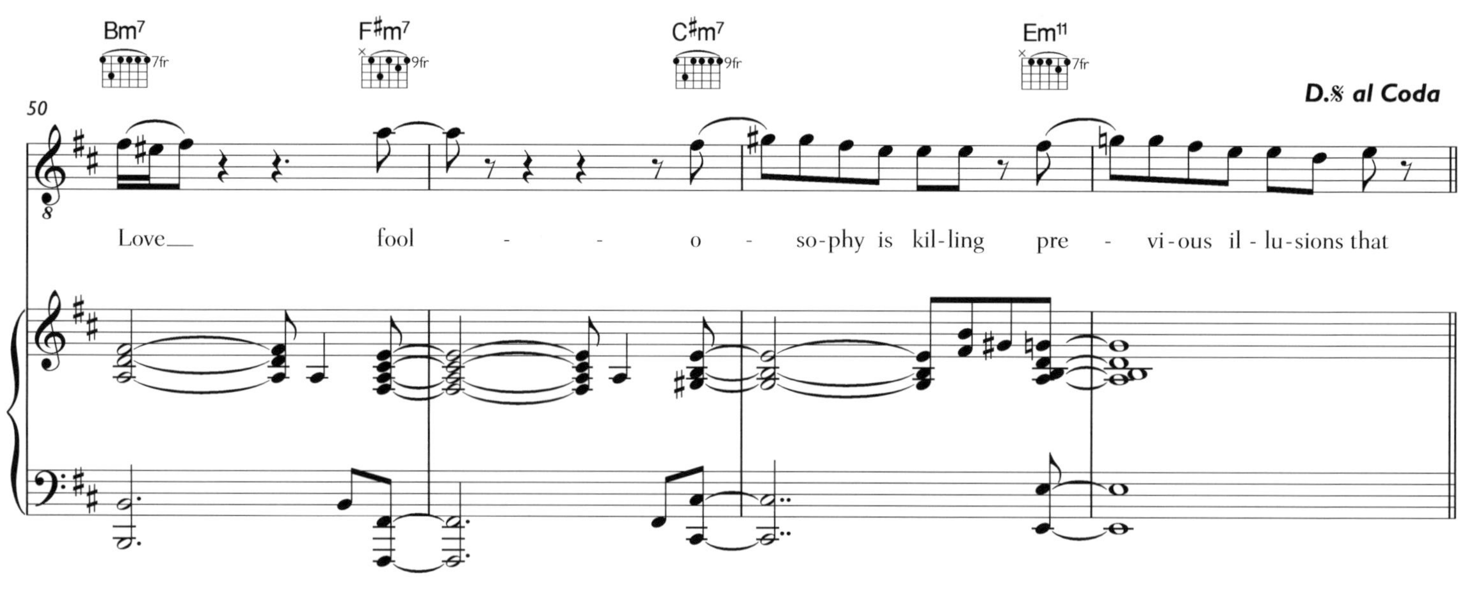
Bm7
F#m7
C#m7
Em11
D.% al Coda
Love___ fool - - o - so-phy is kil-ling pre - vi-ous il - lu-sions that

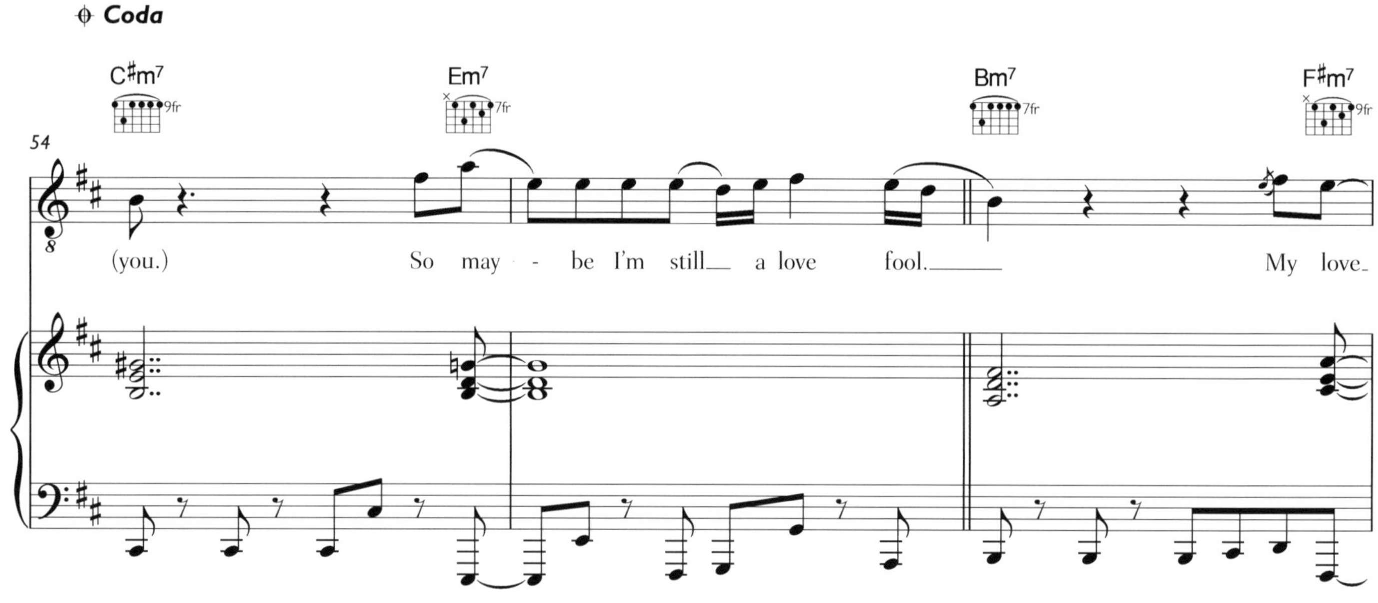
Coda
C#m7
Em7
Bm7
F#m7
(you.) So may - be I'm still___ a love fool.______ My love__

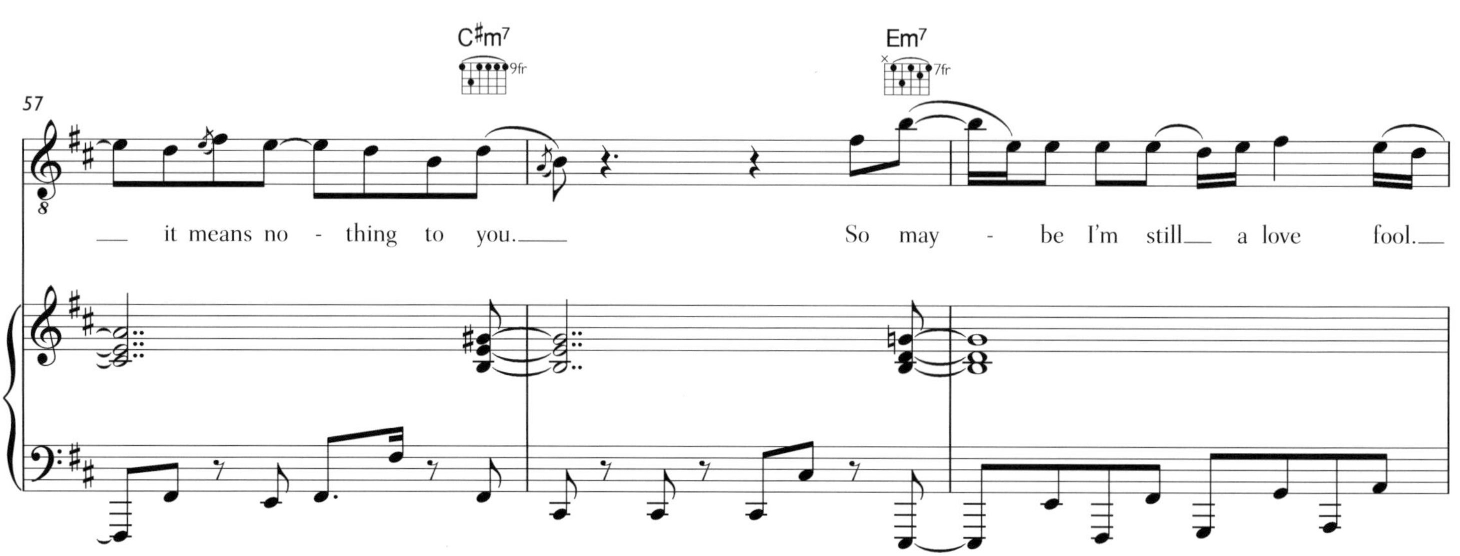
C#m7
Em7
___ it means no - thing to you.___ So may - be I'm still___ a love fool.__

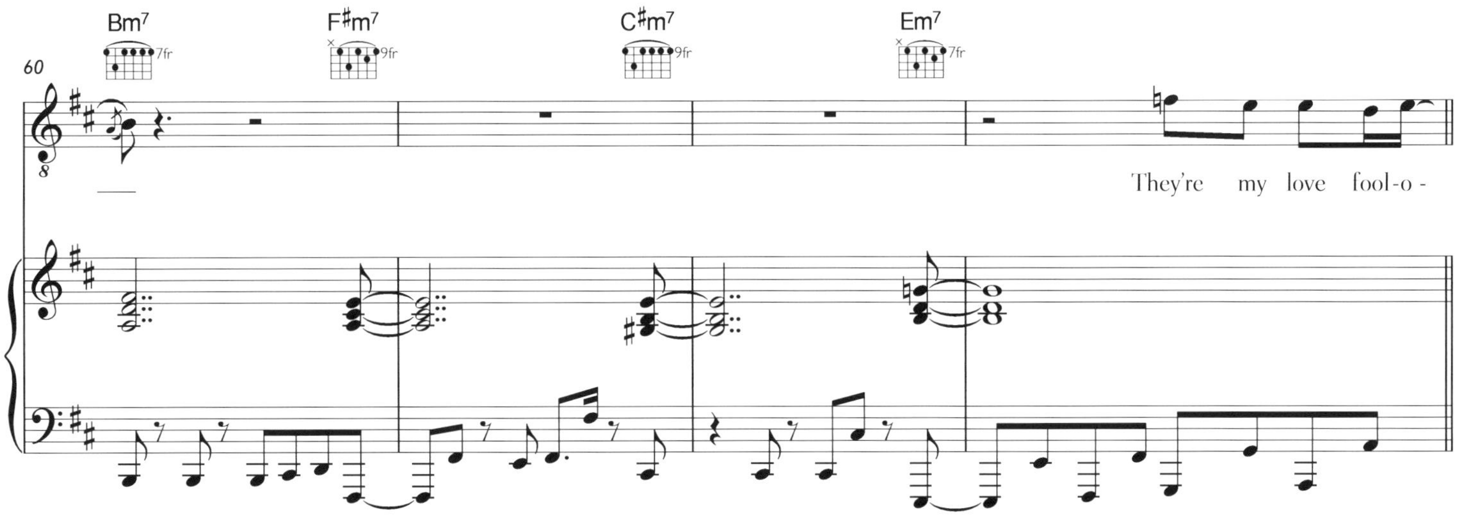
Bm7
7fr
F#m7
9fr
C#m7
9fr
Em7
7fr
60
They're   my   love   fool-o -

Bm7
7fr
F#m7
9fr
C#m7
9fr
Em7
7fr
64
(1° only)
- so-phies,
(2°) yeah,
don't you   see   it's   kil - ling me?
don't you   see they're kil - ling me?
Ooh.

1.
2.
67
N.C.
They're my love fool-o -
I'm   a   love____ fool._

CORNER OF THE EARTH

Words and Music by Jason Kay and Rob Harris

D5 Dm7 D5 Dm7 D5 E♭maj7 E♭6 E♭maj7 E♭6 E♭maj7
If you hur - ry you can get a___ ray___ on you,___________________ come___ with___
The wind it whis-pers and the clouds don't seem to care,_______________ and I___

B♭6 B♭6/9 B♭6 B♭6/9 B♭6 Asus4 A7 A7sus4 A7
me,___ just___ to play.__________________________
know___ in - side_________ that it's all___ mine.__________

Dm7 E♭6/9
Like ev - 'ry hum-ming - bird___ and bum - ble - bee. Ev - 'ry sun - flo - wer, cloud and ev - 'ry tree.
It's the cho - rus of___ the break-ing dawn, the mist that comes___ be - fore the sun is born

B♭6 B♭6/9 B♭6 B♭6/9 B♭6 A7sus4 A7 A7sus4 A7
___ I feel so much a part of this.______
___ to a ha - zy af - ter - noon in May.

D5 Dm7 D5 Dm7 D5 E♭maj7 E♭6 E♭maj7 E♭6 E♭maj7
33
Na - ture's got me high___ and it's beau - ti - ful.___ I'm with this
B♭6 B♭6% B♭6 B♭6% B♭6 Asus4 A7 A7sus4 A7
37
(2° only)
deep e - ter - nal u - ni -verse from death un - til___ re - birth.___ (You know that)
B♭maj7 Gm7 Fmaj7 A7
Guitar rhythm - cont. sim. throughout chorus
41
This cor - ner of the earth is like me in___ ma - ny ways.___ Ah___
mf
B♭maj7 Gm7 Fmaj7 A7
45
I can sit for ho - urs here and watch the em - erald fea -thers play.___

Bbmaj7   Gm7   Fmaj7   A7
On the face of it I'm blessed when the sun-light comes for free,
1.
Bbmaj7   Gm7   Fmaj7   A7   A
I know this cor-ner of the earth it smiles at me.
2.3.
Bbmaj7   Gm7   Fmaj7   A7
To Coda
I know this cor-ner of the earth it smiles at me.
Bbmaj7   Gm7   Fmaj7   A7   A
I know this cor-ner of the earth it smiles at me.

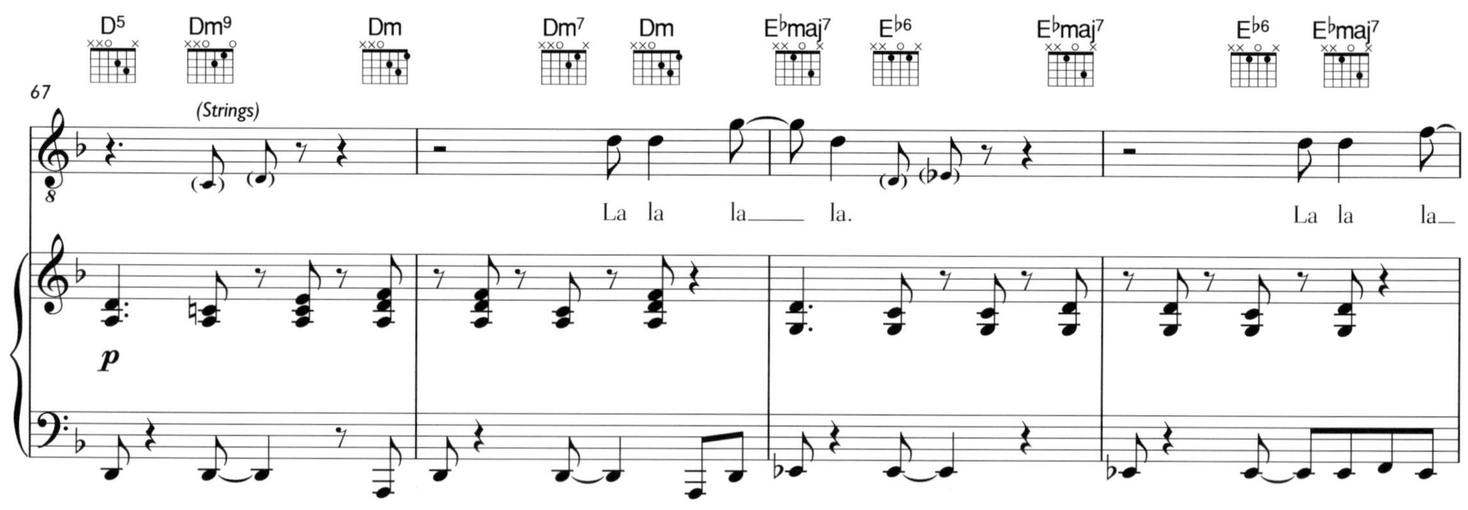
D5   Dm9   Dm   Dm7   Dm   Ebmaj7   Eb6   Ebmaj7   Eb6   Ebmaj7
67
(Strings)
p
La la la___ la.   La la la___

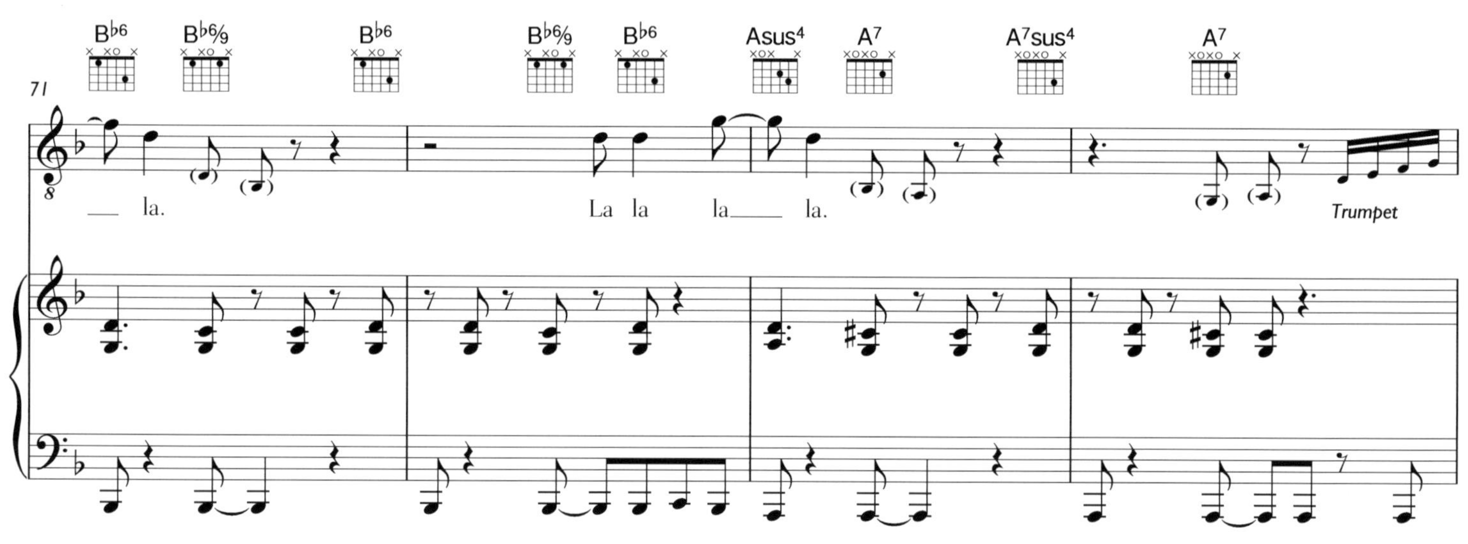
Bb6   Bb6/9   Bb6   Bb6/9   Bb6   Asus4   A7   A7sus4   A7
71
___ la.   La la la___ la.
Trumpet

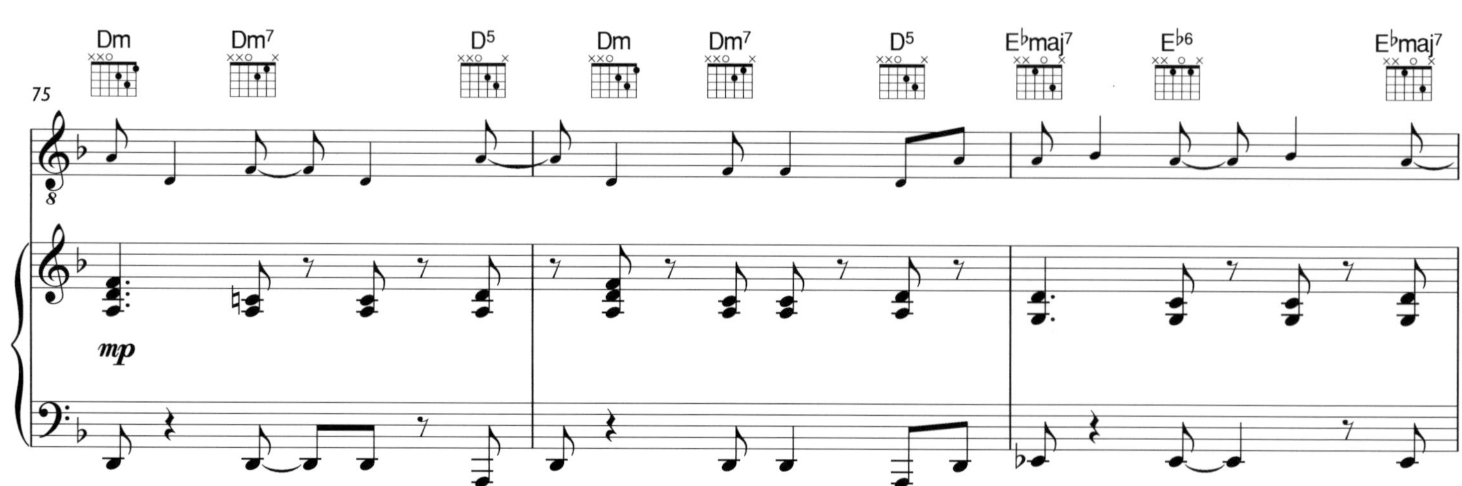
Dm   Dm7   D5   Dm   Dm7   D5   Ebmaj7   Eb6   Ebmaj7
75
mp

93

E♭6   E♭maj7   B♭6   B♭6/9   B♭6   B♭6/9   B♭6
78

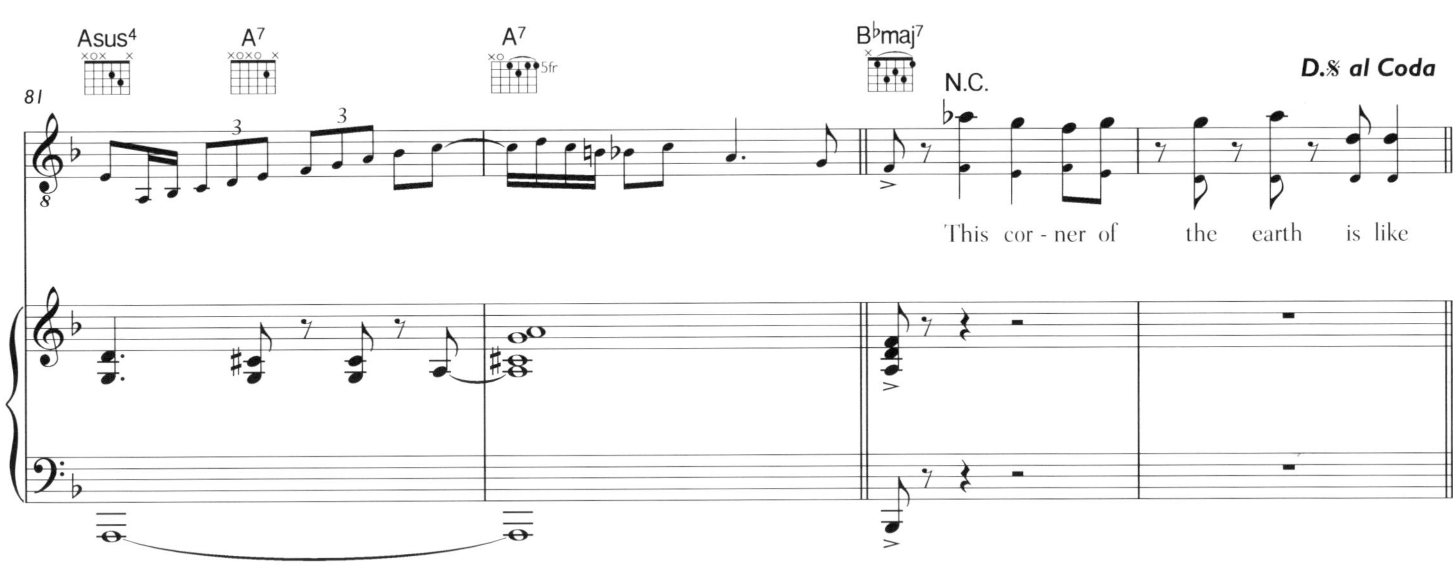
Asus4   A7   A7   B♭maj7   N.C.   D.§ al Coda
81
This cor - ner of   the   earth   is like

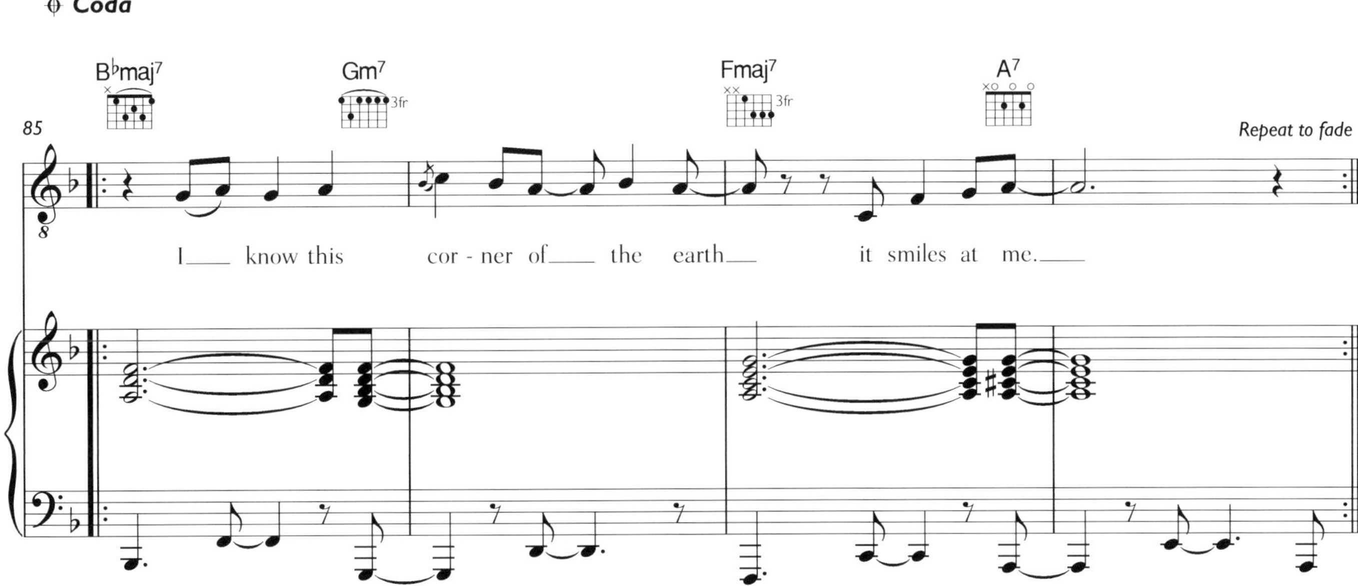
⊕ Coda
B♭maj7   Gm7   Fmaj7   A7
Repeat to fade
85
I___ know this   cor - ner of___ the   earth___   it smiles at me.___

FEELS JUST LIKE IT SHOULD

Words and Music by Jason Kay

I'm gon - na get ex - pe - ri - enced.
So take me for the first_ time.
I'm here to see the can - dy - man._
I need a lit - tle su - gar_ spice. Yeow_____
To turn it up and drown.
I wan - na see the ci - ty lights.
(2° only)
I'm gon - na find a num - ber.
She said
She said
feels_ just like_ it should._
(Yeow.)_
Feels just like_ it should.
ff
8vb
(Yeow.)_____
Feels just like_ it should._
(8)

20
(1° only)
I'm gon-na get ex - pe - ri - enced.   (Yeow.)___   Feels just   like___ it   should.___
(8)
1.   2.
22
Turn it   up and drown.   (should)   I'm look - in' for it   fast___ and cheap.
(8)
8vb
24
Feels just   like___ it   should.___   I'm look-in' for the black moon streets. (Yeow.)___
(8)
26
(Feels_ just   like___ it   should.)___   I'm gon-na get ex - pe - ri - enced.   (Yeow.)___
(8)

28
(Feels just like it should.) I'm here to see the can - dy - man. (Yeow.)
(8)
30
Feels just like it should.
(8)
33
(8)
36 (A) (G#)
Su - gar spice, I'm on the phone, I'm out - side, I need a lit - tle sex - funk a - bout now,
mf (8)
38 (G) (F#) N.C.
I want you, I wan - na lick you up and down, feels good. You said it would feel that good and it does.
(8)

98
Sing main lyrics 2° only
(Sing 1° only)
(feels), it feels, it feels. And it feels,___ it feels, it feels. And it feels, Yeow___
f
8vb
1.
___ it feels, it feels_ just like you, And it feels, Yeow___
(8)
2.
just like you said it would. (Yeow.)___ (Feels_ just like_ it should.)
ff
(8)
(Yeow.) (Feels_just like_ it should.)___ I'm com-in' out_ to-night to taste_y'all.
(8)

49
Su - gar spice, I want_ you, a se - xy girl, slips_ in, it feels good. I love

51
_ it when you tell me._
Feels_ just like_ it should._

53
with ad-lib. spoken vocals
Play section x4

55
Synth.
Repeat to fade
mf

SEVEN DAYS IN SUNNY JUNE

Words and Music by Matthew Richard Johnson and Jason Kay

G13sus4   Am7   F#m7
- stel-la - tions as__ we lie__ here.   There's a ma-gic I___ can__ hold, your smile of ho-ney gold
- mer dress you wore in spring.   The way_ we laughed as__ one, and then you dropped the___
Dm7   G13sus4
___   and that__ you ne - ver seem__ to be_ in short_ sup-ply__ of.
bomb, that I'd_ known you__ too long__ for_ us to have_ a thing.___
Bm7   F#m7   Bm7   F#m7   Fmaj9   Gmaj9
Guitar rhythm - cont. sim. throughout chorus
Ooh,___   so ba-by let's get it on.__   Drink-ing wine__ and kil-ling time__
Amaj9   D7sus4(add2)   Bm7   F#m7   Bm7   F#m7
sit-ting in the sum-mer sun.__   You___ know I've_ want-ed you so long,
mf

Fmaj9
Gmaj9
Amaj9
D7sus4(add2)
1.
Am
why d'you have to drop that bomb on me? La - zy
F#m7
Dm9
G13sus4
Am
days, cra - zy dolls.
You said we'd
F#m7
Dm9
G13sus4
been friends too long.
2.
Bm7
F#m7
Bm7
F#m7
Fmaj9
Gmaj9
Guitar rhythm - cont. sim. throughout chorus
Ooh, so ba-by let's get it on. Drink - ing wine and kil-ling time
mp

Amaj9
D7sus4(add2)
Bm7
F#m7
Bm7
F#m7
sit-ting in the sum-mer sun.. You___ know I've_ want-ed you so long,
Fmaj9
Gmaj9
Amaj9
D7sus4(add2)
Am7
why d'you have to drop that bomb on me? Could it be this? The sto-
mp
Ped.
F#m7
Dm9
- ries in___ your eyes_ tell of si - lent wings you fly a - way___ on. Se-ven
Ped.
Bm7
F#m7
Bm7
F#m7
Guitar rhythm - cont. sim.
days in sun-ny June were long___ e - nough to bloom___

Fmaj9   Gmaj9   Amaj7   D7sus4(add2)   Bm7   F#m7
flo-wers on__ that sun-beam dress you wore__ in__ spring, yeah_ yeah.__ The way we laughed
Bm7   F#m7   Fmaj7   Gmaj7   Amaj7   D7sus4(add2)
as one.   Why did you drop that bomb on me?
Bm7   F#m7   Bm7   F#m7   Fmaj9   Gmaj9
Ooh,__   so ba-by let's get it on.__ Drink-ing wine__ and kil-ling time__
Amaj9   D7sus4(add2)   Bm7   F#m7   Bm7   F#m7
sit-ting in the sum-mer sun.__ You__ know I've_ want-ed you so long.
mf

Fmaj9
Gmaj9
Amaj9
D7sus4(add2)
Bm7
F#m7
Guitar rhythm - cont. sim.
56
Why d'you have to drop that bomb on me? Could it be this? The ho-ney-su - ckle
Bm7
F#m7
Fmaj9
Gmaj9
59
bless-ings seem to show me. Could it be this? For se-ven days in June
Amaj9
D7sus4(add2)
Bm7
F#m7
61
I was-n't lone-ly. Could it be this? You ne-ver gave me time
Bm7
F#m7
Fmaj9
Gmaj9
Amaj9
D7sus4(add2)
63
to say I love you. Could it be this? I know you don't be - lieve me but it's so true.

Bm7   F#m7   Bm7   F#m7   Fmaj9   Gmaj9
Don't walk a-way from me girl,   I read the sto-ries in your eyes.
2° ad-lib. vocals
Amaj9   D7sus4(add2)   Bm7   F#m7   Bm7   F#m7
Don't you walk a-way from me,   I read the sto-ries in your eyes.
Fmaj9   Gmaj9   Amaj9   D7sus4(add2)
And you've been tel-ling me we've been friends for too long.
Bm7   F#m7   Bm7   F#m7   Fmaj9
Guitar rhythm
Ooh.

(DON'T) GIVE HATE A CHANCE

Words and Music by Jason Kay, Matthew Richard Johnson and Rob Harris

F#m
16
des - ti - ny.___ And if you wan - na rise up,
Trig - ger hap - py fan - ta - sy. So___ stand___ up and be
(We got this sin - gle love___ in - side___
(so___ strong
Bm7
Dm7
19
we can make this hate stop.
___ us.)
we can make this hate stop.
___ now.)
Now don't you wan - na rise up?
Bm7
F#
Bm/D
C#m7
B
22
We've been giv - ing hate a chance.
(We got all this love to give,
ff
Amaj7
C#m7
Dmaj7
26
you know.) And the love will be run - ning out for___ us.

E
F#
Bm/D
C#m7
B
Can you feel the dreams of life?___ We're hop-ing we can still sur-vive___
Amaj7
C#m7 Dmaj7
To Coda
as the wind car-ries ev-'ry dove a - way.___
1.
2.
Amaj7
2. So
The wind car-ries ev-'ry dove
C#m7 Dmaj7
E
___ a - way.___ The wind car-ries ev-'ry dove___ a - way.___ Ev-'ry dove a-

F#
D6
C#m7
B
D6
mf
- way.)
Now you've been___ tak - ing___
C#m7
B
D6
C#m7
B
our dig - ni - ty___ for too___ long.
I want to___ save this___
D6
C#m7
B
D6
C#m7
B
D6
sanc - ti - ty___ that we___ hold.
And who's right___ and who is wrong?___
C#m7
B
D6
C#m7
We're not so dif - ferent a - ny - way.
Words are___ in

B
D6
C#m7
B
D.%. al Coda
this song.___
Can't we stop the fight-ing 'cause we've been giv-ing
Coda
Dmaj7
E
F#
Bm/D
C#m7
(Don't give this hate a chance, we've got
B
Amaj7
all this love to give. You know that this dream's a - live, we'll
Repeat & ad lib. to fade
C#m7
Dmaj7
E
still sur - vive un - til no more peo - ple have to cry. I say)

RUNAWAY

Words and Music by Matthew Richard Johnson,
Jason Kay and Rob Harris

C7 C7 Ab Fm6 C7 C7
wan - na ride?
go - ing in - sane?
Got to make it,
I wan - na be a free man,
Ab Fm6 C7 C7 Ab Fm6
make it to the o - ther side.
but I'm spin - ning on this cra - zy wheel.
I've got de -
I'm jump - ing for the
C7 C7 Ab Fm6 C7 C7
- mons
high bar, can't you dig it?
snap - ping at my heels to - night.
No long - er know what I feel.
Ab Fm6 C5
(2° only)
Gmaj7 Abmaj7
Can't you see I just want to run a - way.
f

G+7 Fmaj7
E+7
25
Turn me loose.   I got peo-ple a - round,___   grind-ing me down,___

Eb6   D7   Dbmaj9   C5   Gmaj7
28
I can't stay.   I   just___   want   to___

Abmaj7   G+7   Fmaj7
32
get a-way.   I just wan-na get a - way___ now.   Get   them___
Turn me loose.

E+7   Eb6   1.   D7   Dbmaj9
35
off   my___   back to- day.   2. Can you   feel

2.3.
D7   Dbmaj9   To Coda   C5
38
I just wan-na run a - way.   Ah.   Ah.
C9sus4   Cm7   Cm9   Gm7#5
41
Ah.   Ah.
mp cresc.
Abmaj7   F7/A   G7/B   C9sus4   Cm7
45
Got to make it.   Got to make
Cm9   Gm7#5   Abmaj7   F7/A   G7/B   D.% al Coda
48
it,   got to make it,   got to make it.

⊕ Coda

C5
Gmaj7 A♭maj7
1. (way)   I just wan-na get a - way.______   Turn me loose.
2. (way)   I just got to get a - way.______
La la   la__ la la la.   La la   la__ la la la.
G+7 Fmaj7   E+7
(1° only)
Run a - way.______   I got peo-ple a - round__   grind-ing me down,__
Run a - way.______   Get____ them____   off____ my____
E♭6   D7   D♭maj9
(1° only)
I can't stay.__   Run-ning a - way.   Run-ning a - way   I just wan-na run a - way
back to-day.__   3
1.
2.
D7   D♭maj9   N.C.
Ah.____
6

RADIO

**Words and Music by Matthew Richard Johnson,
Jason Kay, Rob Harris and Derrick McKenzie**

F#m7(add4)
Dm7
- thing she can't dis - guise from me.
D7sus2
B7sus4
Bm7
B7sus4
Guitar chord rhythm follows keyboard part - cont. sim.
1. Two lov - ing whis-pers from her black - ened lips___ was all it took to get a
2. some fun - ny mo - ney fun-ny bus-iness go-ing on. Some-thing she's keep-ing from me,
(Bass guitar fills - 2° only)
Bm7
F#m7
F#7sus2
F#m7
F#7sus2
C#7sus4
touch, feel, kiss. Now she's gone.___ I'm left a - lone, lone like a load - ed gun.
I'm not dumb, don't give a damn.___ Well three's___ not a crowd. I'm a
C#m7
C#7sus4
C#m7
Dm7
D7sus2
Dm7
I see you soon Let's have some fun. Let's get it on.___ I have a reef - er and some
man. I'm a man. She likes___ boys,___

D7sus2
B7sus4
Bm7
B7sus4
Bm7
F#m7
Spa-nish ci-ga-rettes, and on the back was writ-ten her ad - dress. Call me up,
she_ likes girls, twists her lit-tle fin - gers round those supernatural curls. There's a spi -
F#7sus2
F#m7
F#7sus2
C#7sus4
C#m7
C#7sus4
- der in her eyes. try me on,_ tune me in._ Let's make a su-per - no - va, let's
Some-thing she can't dis-guise. That girl,_ oh she's
C#m7
Dm9
Guitar ends
Bm7
make a-no-ther nak - ed light_ show. Let's get it on the ra - di - o._
mak - ing_ love in_ ste-re-o.
mf
F#m9
C#m9
You took me last night and you weren't a - lone._ Let's get it on the ra - di - o._

Dm9
Bm7
F#m9
C#m9
Am
F#7sus4
Am7
35
You're mak - ing love to me   in ste - re - o.
1. Let's do some cra - zy   shit   to - night.
2. Let's sneak it on the   mid - night   news.
39
You guys have got the on - ly   tune I   like.
You liked it once but now you   work in   twos.
So____ let's get it on the   ra - di - o.____ Just
Guitar chord rhythm follows right-hand keyboard part - cont. sim.
To Coda
43
do it to me, give it to me, mak - ing love in ste - re - o.   Well you come un - stuck when you got mis -
f
47
-in - for - ma - tion. Don't drop me   now,____   I'm high.   You dropped my le - ver and I

F#7sus4
Dm7
Am7
lost this e - le - va - tion.___ Oh ba - by you're wrong. All night.
Ba - by I was so high, drop me out of your sky.
F#7sus4
Dm7
You were ma - king love to me in ste - re - o. Can't you see___ there's no - thing wrong.
D.%. al Coda
Am7
F#7sus4
Dm7
All night. I know you wan - na get it on the ra - di - o. 2. That's when
Am
F#7sus4
Coda
Guitar chord rhythm follows right-hand keyboard part - cont. sim.
mak - ing love in ste - re - o. All night, all night, all night, let's get it on.__
ff

64
Am7
F#7sus4
All night, all night, let's just get it on.
all night

68
Dm7
Am7
F#7sus4
Hey, I know all a - long you were mak - ing love to me in

72
Dm7
Am7
ste - re - o. I can see there's no-thing wrong. I

75
F#7sus4
Dm7
know you wan - na get it on the ra - di - o. Oh let's get it on.
All

night,   all night,   let's just get it on.____   All
night,   all night,   all night,   let's get it on.______
All
Some-thing she's keep - ing from me,___ I'm not dumb._
I don't give a damn.___   Three's not a crowd,   I'm a man,   I'm a man.